G

Missions,

AND A MAN

GOD, *Missions,* AND A MAN

A young woman's remarkable journey to know Christ and make Him known.

KRISTINE AKANA

Published by Reliant Publishing, and imprint of Redemption Press, PO Box 427, Enumclaw, WA 98022.

Toll-Free (844) 2REDEEM (273-3336)

Redemption Press is honored to present this title in partnership with the author. The views expressed or implied in this work are those of the author. Redemption Press provides our imprint seal representing design excellence, creative content, and high-quality production.

ISBN: 978-1-64645-173-9 (Paperback)
978-1-64645-174-6 (ePub)
978-1-64645-175-3 (Mobi)

Library of Congress Catalog Card Number: 2020908043

This book is dedicated to…

David—*Jesus loves you, and I am able to love you with His love.*

My parents—*Thank you for believing in God's calling.*

My Haitian children—*You are always in my heart.*

My nieces and nephews—*I love you! Always look to the One who loves you with an everlasting love.*

Contents

Introduction

You are holding a book that will take you on adventures across the ocean, invite you into the secret place of my home, and share with you the darkest night of my life. In a way you are holding my heart in your hands. I have always loved reading stories of people whose simple faith in Christ moved insurmountable mountains. What an adventurous life they lived and what stories they could share! It became my dream to share about the greatness of our God.

You will quickly see that I am an imperfect vessel, and my hope is that through these adventures, mountains, and valleys, you will see the masterful Author who walked on earth as our perfect example (Hebrews 12:2). I hope that you will see His boundless love for you that reaches to the heavens (Psalm 36:5). I pray that as you join me on the dusty streets of Léogâne and on the beaches of O'ahu, you will be transformed as I was by an encounter with the living God. This is a story about *God—my salvation; missions—my calling; a man—to love.*

We have this hope as an anchor for the soul, firm and secure.
It enters into the inner sanctuary
behind the curtain.
Hebrews 6:9

Chapter One

Screaming in Desperation

Lord, You have given us the name Christian;
now give us strength to carry it.
A HAITIAN PRAYER

The truck jolted, and I opened my eyes as a gunman with a bandanna over his face approached our pickup, motioning for the driver to roll down his window. The sweltering Haitian heat flooded through the opened window. Without time to process, I turned to my right, and life began to move in slow motion. Another man approached our vehicle and motioned his pistol in a circle—a silent but clear command. Without hesitation I obeyed.

I gazed at the dashboard in front of me, sensing the metal of the handgun near my head. My breathing became shallow as my chest tightened. Frozen in place, I held my head high as my eyes shifted into tunnel vision. *What do they want?* I thought about my children in Léogâne and my family in Minnesota. *Will I ever see them again?*

My numbed senses immediately snapped back. Without moving, I slowly shifted my eyes to my left. The driver frantically pulled out dollar bills and *gourdes* (Haitian currency) onto his lap, then turned his pockets inside out. The gunman snatched up his plunder. Suddenly the weight of my cell phone lifted from my lap. *Will he be satisfied? What if they abduct me?* I sat painfully still and slowly shifted my eyes to my right. I could see only the top portion of my captor's face. His dark eyes were inches from mine. I memorized his features and read his eyes intently. They were screaming—screaming out in desperation.

I wondered if bystanders were taking cover, but I dared not observe what was happening outside the truck. I wanted to disappear—to become invisible to our captors. But I wasn't invisible; I was wholly in their presence.

Suddenly their shadows shifted as they stepped back and away from the front of the pickup. We waited several moments. Then, without warning, my driver slammed on the gas. Moments after our escape, loud gunshots sounded. I ducked, wondering if they were shooting at us, at bystanders, or at the sky in defiance. *Were we allowed to leave? Or had my driver made this erratic decision?*

As we raced down the street, I turned to my alarmed chauffeur. His hands squeezed the steering wheel, and he was leaning forward, as if his posture would help us speed away faster. His eyes stared with intense concentration as he drove frantically down the street.

I tried to catch my breath and spewed out in Haitian Creole, *"Paspò mwen nan sachèm. M'konnen yo te prann li!"* (My passport is in my backpack, and I know that they took it!)

My driver's face morphed into a look of annoyance as he continued clenching the wheel with his left hand and stared down the road. His right hand moved up and down from the steering wheel as he explained that I should always keep my passport on me. As he lectured, my mind drifted off. *How will I get home?* I thought about having to go to the U.S. Embassy. *How long will I be here before I'm allowed to leave? Where will I stay as I wait for a new passport?*

Suddenly I felt the truck slow down as we turned and pulled into the airport terminal. Just as we stopped, I quickly jumped out of my seat and rushed to the back of the truck. I stood at the rear of the pickup and stared in disbelief at my backpack, sitting right where I had left it. *Why hadn't they taken it?* I didn't have time for questions, and I grabbed for it. My translator reassured me that all my belongings remained in the bag.

"They were going to take it," my translator Sonson relayed to me wide-eyed. "But I told them, 'You cannot take this bag!'"

I nodded, shocked that it was in my hands, not theirs.

"Mèsi, zanmi'm." (Thank you, my friend.) I refocused my attention and walked toward the airport entrance. Airport security greeted me at the entryway and scanned my bag as I walked through the metal detector. I went to the front counter to receive my flight documents and handed my passport to the agent at the counter.

My eyes felt glazed over. She casually handed me my boarding pass and sent me on my way. I tried to smile back, although I'm not sure I succeeded.

"Mèsi," I mumbled, and then walked to the lobby.

I spotted a cushioned chair, walked over to it, and sat down. Leaning my head back, I closed my eyes and tried to process what had just happened. *Lord, thank You for Your protection.* I had heard of the real nightmare of Americans being abducted in Port-au-Prince for ransom. I also knew that traveling in Haiti as a single Caucasian female was risky, but I always believed that the Lord would protect me. In fact, it seemed as if I had a supernatural covering over me that made my belongings and body invisible to the bandits.

I clenched my backpack closer to my chest with my invaluable passport in hand. Psalm 91:1 flashed into my mind: "Whoever dwells in the shelter of the Most High will abide in the shadow of the Almighty." Perhaps I wasn't invisible—but in the shadow of my God. I breathed in deeply, with a new appreciation for His protection and the precious opportunity to live.

Jim and Elisabeth Elliot came to mind, great heroes of the faith. *Were they prepared for death on the day that Jim was speared?* Their goal in Ecuador was to share the gospel with an unreached, indigenous tribe—the hostile Aucas. Their team members had made friendly contact from an airplane, but when Jim and four other missionaries landed and approached the villagers, they were speared to death. Jim was twenty-eight years old—a couple of years older than me—when he was martyred by people he loved for a message that embodied the greatest love.

What I found even more incredible about the Elliots' story was Elisabeth's return to the tribe, taking along her ten-month-old daughter. They lived and served the Auca people for two more years. Jim and Elisabeth Elliot became an inspiration to thousands because of their bold and authentic faith.

Along those lines, Jim once said, "He is no fool who gives that which he cannot keep to gain that which he cannot lose." He believed in a message for which he laid down his life. This message was so deep that it had eternal significance, yet so simple even a child could understand it. As the children's song says, "Jesus loves me! This I know, for the Bible tells me so."

My thoughts turned once again, drifting back to reality as I opened my eyes and took notice of my surroundings. The airport was swarming with people preparing to leave Haiti for other places. As I watched people pass by, gratitude filled my heart. I loved Haiti, but the safety of U.S. soil had never sounded better. I thought about getting to see my family again—an experience Jim Elliot wasn't given. Yet Jim's selfless act of love for others provided an opportunity for hundreds of Aucas to give their lives to Christ. He lived out what Paul said in Philippians 1:21, "For to me, to live is Christ and to die is gain."

I knew that Jesus was worth my life—but this was something I hadn't always believed.

Reflection

- Do you think sharing the gospel is worth risking your life?

- What do you think about those who've given their lives for the gospel?

____

____

____

____

____

____

____

____

____

____

____

____

Meditation

> Go into all the world and proclaim the gospel to the whole creation (Mark 16:15).
>
> And I heard the voice of the LORD saying, "Whom shall I send, and who will go for us?" Then I said, "Here I am! Send me" (Isaiah 6:8).
>
> Therefore go and make disciples of all nations, baptizing them in the name of the Father and of the Son and of the Holy Spirit (Matthew 28:19 NIV).

Chapter Two
Who's First?

You shall have no other gods before me.
Exodus 20:3

As my ten-year-old self yawned and stretched out on my parents' bed, my dad read the Bible to my brothers and me. Though powerful, this Creator my dad spoke of seemed distant, as if He existed only on the ruffled pages of his Bible. I didn't understand how these ancient stories related to me. But one thing was certain: Every story ended with the same predictable theme—*Jesus loves me.* Yet I didn't understand *how* He loved me.

Just as predictably, church on Sundays smelled like the old wooden pews where I casually dozed off as the pastor preached on in his soothing voice. However, one time at the end of his message he started to talk about sinners going to a place of eternal fire. Fear gripped me as I imagined being tormented there. I followed his lead as he led the congregation in a prayer. I had prayed, but this path seemed safe and predictable—and I craved something more.

One weekend I joined my best friend Tina and her family on a camping trip. In the evening, rain and thunder shook the camper. The adults rushed out to take care of something. Without hesitation, Tina and I snatched their beer and took a swig. The taste was pungent, and I quickly spit it out. But in that moment, the intoxicating rush of rebellion began to course through my veins. Tina and I formed a clan with a few other students. Our peers labeled us as druggies—perhaps because they thought our rebellion included drugs. Or maybe it was their way of denoting a negative connotation to our behavior. Either way, we didn't care.

One day in school, as we sat and ate at the lunch table, the lunch lady spoke to us in a voice just above a whisper: "Please stop throwing your food."

"We're just bouncing cheese," we piped back. "It's not a big deal!" We turned our backs to her.

Tears began to fall down her face. "No one has ever made me cry before," she said through her sobs.

Later that day, the principal called us into his office and gave us detention slips. I carefully practiced and forged my mom's signature and returned the slip, ready to serve my time during lunch without my parents' awareness.

Another time, our math teacher kept us after class. As he raised his voice, we laughed in defiance. And later that school year, our seasoned geography teacher told us we were by far the worst class she'd ever had the displeasure to teach.

My friends and I were given several detentions and scoldings throughout our middle school career, but these mild chastisements didn't faze us. I felt empowered, and the sense of autonomy was exhilarating.

After lunch one day, my middle school friends gathered outside the cafeteria. They scanned the area to make sure the hall monitors were out of earshot. I knew they were going to formulate a plan to obtain marijuana, but I didn't understand why we needed to be stoned to have fun. It didn't make sense to be chained to a mind-altering substance when I could run and be free.

I had recently joined the track team, and in competitions, the sensation of my spikes touching the track tarmac for a split second was more than exhilarating. When I received a prized medal or found tenths of a second shaved off my previous race time, I was given something that drugs couldn't give—victory. And victory was possible only with camaraderie. My teammates and I forged an alliance to reach our goal and defeat our competitors.

In high school, I drifted from my middle school friends and developed new friendships. My new friends were fun and goal-oriented, but God wasn't our focus, and we eventually slipped into tempting vices. Lying to our parents and drinking alcohol became our idea of amusement.

One day at school, Erica—my soft-spoken, loyal friend—invited me to a Christian youth conference. I accepted her invitation and thought about the great time we would have running around, rocking out to concerts, and doing other crazy things.

At the conference, we jumped around and cheered with the crowd. Then right after the last song finished, a man walked out on stage.

He grabbed the live mic and stated, "God needs to be number one in your life."

I caught my breath as his words unexpectedly cut like daggers into my conscience. I knew that God wasn't first priority in my life. In fact, into my adolescence, He still seemed to exist only in church, the Bible, and perhaps a quick prayer before meals.

The speaker continued, and my rebellious lifestyle flashed before my eyes. Partying with friends and living precariously from one rebellious event to another was freeing—*wasn't it?* My conscience reasoned excuses, but it couldn't get away from the deep and precise cuts of conviction.

Was I really free? When I lied once, it would lead to another and another. And being sick the entire day after consuming immeasurable amounts of alcohol with my friends the night before wasn't exactly invigorating. *But isn't it my right to blaze a trail and lead my life?* The more I reasoned, the less weight it carried. And the more I listened to what the speaker said, the more my stomach turned. I tried to justify my past behavior, but now somehow, I understood that my lies, drunkenness, and idolatry were all a source of great evil against my Creator.

The speaker continued, "Your sin separates you from God, but Jesus died for the sins of the world. If you're willing to turn from your sin and turn to Him, He will forgive you."

After the speaker finished, I could hear a pin drop in the large sanctuary filled with teens. Waves of conviction continued to batter my heart. I had heard many times from my parents that Jesus died on a cross for my sins, but I never understood the gravity of my sin—until now.

Suddenly a Bible verse I had memorized as a young child flashed into my mind: "For God so loved the world that He gave his one and only Son so that whoever believes in Him will not perish but have eternal life" (John 3:16). Tears flooded my eyes. *What kind of love would pursue me in the dark trenches of rebellion and sin? How could He love me when I'd wronged Him over and over again?*

I closed my eyes and imagined His torn and bloodied body all alone on the cross. The familiar Bible story theme didn't seem mundane anymore: *Jesus loves me.* I closed my eyes, desperate for forgiveness. *Lord, forgive me for not putting You, my Creator, first. Please forgive me of my sins.*

In that moment, I recognized that He wasn't distant. I knew that He listened to every word I silently and desperately prayed. I turned to Erica with tear-stained eyes.

"I'm not living like this anymore," I said.

"Me neither," she responded.

We walked out of the auditorium. My tears dried, and a deep resolve settled into my soul. God would be first now. My life was no longer about me; it would be about Him.

At school the following week, Erica extended another invitation. She told me about a teacher, Kelly Citrowske, who led a weekly youth Bible study for girls. Later that week, we showed up to her study at a local Bible church.

Kelly began, "The doctrine of the Trinity is difficult to wrap our minds around. But if we deny the Trinity, the Bible becomes incomprehensible and contradictory. Let's dive in! John 1:1 says, 'In the beginning was the Word, and the Word was with God, and the Word was God.'" Kelly drew a triangle on a whiteboard with three points: the Father, Son, and Holy Spirit.

She seemed to have a bright light in her eyes as she continued.

"In the beginning, God created the heavens and the earth. God said, 'Let us make man in our image, after our likeness' (Genesis 1:26). Notice the plurality God uses for Himself. Then He declares in Deuteronomy 6:4, 'Hear O Israel: The LORD our God, the LORD is one.' And in Revelation 1:8, Jesus says of Himself, 'I am the Alpha and the Omega, who is, and who was, and who is to come, the Almighty'—these are all descriptions of God. And in verse 18 of Revelation 1, Jesus says, 'I am He who lives, and was dead, and behold, I am alive forevermore.' Consider this: If Jesus was just a man, then how did He defeat death?"

I sat back and considered that if Jesus had never risen from the grave, He would have been just a man, not God. Therefore, He wouldn't have been able to conquer death and have victory over sin. Christianity in essence would just be a religion, powerless to offer true forgiveness and eternal life.

I reflected on the radical transformation I had recently experienced. It was as if I had been colorblind, but now I could see everything in vibrant colors. As if scales were removed from my eyes, I could see the vileness of my sin and at the same time the beautiful work of salvation and the cleansing that resulted. I no longer desired to poison my body with alcohol or to deceive my parents. My priorities and desires shifted.

Knowing that my Savior had bled and died for me, how could I not give Him my entire life?

Reflection

- Is God number one in your life? If so, how? Are you attending a church that teaches God's Word? What have you learned this week about God?

- How have your friends and peers impacted your desire to know and follow God?

Meditation

For by grace you have been saved through faith. And this is not your own doing; it is the gift of God (Ephesians 2:8).

If you confess with your mouth, "Jesus is Lord," and believe in your heart that God raised Him from the dead, you will be saved (Romans 10:9 NIV).

And Peter said to them, "Repent and be baptized every one of you in the name of Jesus Christ for the forgiveness of your sins, and you will receive the gift of the Holy Spirit" (Acts 2:38).

Chapter Three
Sex, Purity, and Relationships

There is dullness, monotony, sheer boredom in all of life when virginity and purity are no longer protected and prized.
(Elisabeth Elliot)

My high school days brought some times of confusion.

As we ran indoors for track because of inclement weather, an upperclassman hung out in the doorway. As I went by, he said an inappropriate comment. I grimaced and shook my head. *Why does he do this to me?* He'd said weird things to me before, but I always tried to brush him off and not let his comments get to me.

Tyler, my brother, ran in track as well, and he overheard the upperclassman's comment. He immediately confronted him. Though I was out of earshot, I stopped and looked ahead, watching to see what would happen. Suddenly, Tyler grabbed the guy's books and folders and tossed them to the floor. I held my breath, wondering what Tyler would do next. Just then a teacher appeared, saw what was going on, and stopped the ensuing fight. I smiled, thankful for my brother's willingness to defend me.

One day at school, a friend told me that her mom had "the talk" with her. "She told me I had to start taking the pill," my friend said, shrugging her shoulders. I didn't know how to respond. I wondered why her mom had assumed my friend was having sex, and why she would provide her with something that might actually encourage her to do so.

One time in class, a girl stated with absolute certainty that it would be better to live with your partner before getting married. "That way," she said, "you can really get to know each other before being committed to marriage."

I didn't know it at the time—neither did she—that statistically those who live together before marriage have a higher likelihood of divorce than those who wait until marriage to live together. In fact, a research group conducted a study among several countries in Europe and concluded, "In all countries, the increase in divorce preceded or coincided with the increase in cohabitation."[1]

Although I came to recognize that the true implications of sex were misunderstood by me and those around me, I couldn't pinpoint what exactly was being twisted or misconceived. We needed to be taught and guided; otherwise, society would gladly mislead our young and impressionable minds.

After school, I was busy with track practice or track events or attending a Bible study, and I didn't have time for much else, including a relationship. I wasn't interested in becoming emotionally entangled with a guy when we still had our whole lives ahead of us. My guy friends were just that—friends. I did, however, feel a driving force to know more about what it meant to be a follower of Christ.

Eager to dive in deeper, I went to the local bookstore one day and scanned the variety of Christian titles on the shelves. I floated over to the relationship section and stared wide-eyed at the books in front of me. Falling in love sounded both magical and mysterious.

The bright cover of *Sex Has a Price Tag* caught my eye. I grabbed for the book. If sex has a price, what was that cost? I read the back cover: "Sex is glorious. Sex is God-given. But sex outside God's boundary has far-reaching consequences—a price tag of incalculable costs."[2]

How could having sex have an incalculable price? I skimmed the book's first few pages. "This book is an attempt to offer you both good advice about sex (based on my own personal belief that God is the Creator of the entire universe and everything in it, including sex) and solid information to back it up (based on the latest statistics to come out of the medical community)."[3] I was convinced, and I felt that the author needed to teach me, to mentor me.

Later, as a light breeze coursed past the window curtains, I lay stretched out on my bed with Pam Stenzel's book in my hand. I dove into her book, and as I consumed her message, her words cut with precision through my superficial reasoning and beliefs to reach my soul—the depths of who I am. My mind began forming the concept that sex—a beautiful creation designed by God between one man and one woman in the context of marriage would be utterly marred outside the bonds of marriage. She wrote: "No matter who it's with, no matter how careful you are, you will pay, because there will be consequences immediate and long-term."[4]

Sexual fornication—sex between people not married to each other—creates a web of far-reaching consequences. The staggering list of sexually transmitted infections (STI) seems endless. More than thirty different bacteria, viruses, and parasites can be transmitted through sexual activity.[5] Some can be treated with antibiotics, while others are untreatable. Some of these infections are noticeable because of symptoms, including burning with urination, warts, discharge, or odor. Other STIs are symptomless but still extremely contagious.

I learned from Pam's book that the emotional damage of sexual fornication can be haunting. In the media, when it's insinuated that people have participated in sexual immorality, there's usually no display afterward of fear, shame, regret, or insecurity. Yet all those emotions are a reality in the real world full of people with real hearts and emotions. And certainly, none of this pain is worth celebrating. Tremendous fear of pregnancy, fear of being caught, or fear of being discovered are all part of this web of terror. So are regret, emotional trauma, and haunting memories from the past.

I learned furthermore that sexual immorality cheats a future spouse out of a beautiful gift that was supposed to be meant only for him or her. They're robbed, and they feel the seething pain of loss. Moreover, according to Institute for Family Studies, premarital sex substantially increases the odds for divorce.[6]

As I read about these consequences, my stomach turned, and my throat felt heavy. *Why weren't people teaching my peers and me about this? Why were we left on our own to make choices about sex without being fully informed?* I imagined an unplanned pregnancy. I imagined carrying a disease and passing it on to my future husband. I pictured explaining to him and apologizing for my actions. *No, no, no,* I thought. *This is too much.* The cost did indeed seem incalculable.

As with any story filled with conflict, difficulty, and turmoil, the book took a drastic turn as Pam explained that if we choose to engage in sex the way God intended—exclusively in the context of marriage—we'll be blessed again and again and protected from great harm.

God's design and boundaries are not meant to ruin our lives but to protect and bless us. On the blissful honeymoon night, for the first time, the newly married couple is meant to enter into the deepest level of intimacy. Sex binds the married couple together—physically, mentally, emotionally, and spiritually. This bond creates a soul tie meant to hold them together like glue, which brings closeness and fluidity in life. If the sperm meets the egg, a child begins to develop, and whether he or she is planned or unplanned, that child is a gift from God.

Enjoying sex without worrying about someone walking in, never contracting an STI and passing it on, living regret-free, and living without haunting memories is the life God wants to give us.

While the consequences of sexual immorality seemed overwhelming, the blessings of purity sounded incredible. God has given mankind free will, and He doesn't force anyone to live by the pattern of sexual abstinence until marriage and faithfulness in marriage. But I was learning from this book that if we choose to fornicate, we won't be able to choose the results or consequences.

I sensed a frankness in the author's message as she went on to explain what abstinence would cost: self-denial when emotions and hormones are raging, and the possibility of being perceived as odd and getting teased or ridiculed for it. But she explained that if a virgin is teased by sexually promiscuous people, the fact is that the one practicing abstinence can decide at any time to be like the others, while they can never become like him or her. Virginity lost can never be regained. Virginity is a precious gift we can offer a sexual partner only once, and that one-time gift was meant to be given on the best day of our life: our wedding day.

Furthermore, becoming one flesh with someone outside of marriage comes with a curse. As 1 Corinthians 6:16 says, "Or do you not know that he who is joined to a prostitute becomes one body with her? For, as it is written, 'The two will become one flesh.'" A piece of identity, a sense of self, and a sense of purpose are given away and lost. There's no such thing as casual sex.

I finally set the book down. Reading these thoughts had caused sharp daggers to strike my conscience. I breathed in deeply, knowing I had a decision to make. The repercussions of sexual immorality were clear, and the blessings of waiting were also crystal clear.

Pam encouraged her readers to write out a commitment. Eagerly I grabbed my journal and a pen, and I began writing out my commitment—not only to my future husband but also to God and to myself. With blue ink, I wrote:

> I will be pure. I will save myself for my husband. I will trust in the Lord with all of my heart; I will not lean on my own understanding, and the Lord will direct my paths. I will look into my handsome husband's eyes and say, "Do you know much I love you? Enough to wait for you. You are the first and only person I will ever know sexually."

I signed and dated the paper. I looked at the page in my journal and joy filled my heart as I imagined giving this one day to my future husband.

I continued my study of purity in God's Word. I discovered that purity is interwoven throughout the entire Bible. When God created Eve from Adam's rib and presented her to him, Adam immediately expressed a poem to declare his love: "This at last is bone of my bone and flesh of my flesh; she shall be called Woman, because she was taken out of Man" (Genesis 2:23).

As this very first love story unfolds, we see that God created Adam and Eve to be in a covenantal marriage relationship. In this covenant between husband and wife, they were given the right and blessing to become one flesh through sexual union: "Therefore a man shall leave his father and his mother and hold fast to his wife, and they shall become one flesh. And the man and his wife were both naked and were not ashamed" (Genesis 2:24-25). Their love for one another was untainted. They were innocent and felt no shame. There were no consequences and no regrets. Their story portrayed love in its truest form.

As I continued my study through the pages of the Old Testament, I learned of a people whom God had chosen for Himself. God established a covenant with a man named Abram and told him, "I will surely bless you, and I will surely multiply your offspring as the stars of heaven and as the sand that is on the seashore" (Genesis 22:17). God changed this man's name to Abraham, and through him the Jewish race was created. God promised Abraham that the land of Canaan (later known as Israel) would belong to the Jews. He promised also that ultimately a Messiah would come through Abraham's lineage.

The Jews lived under a theocracy, which meant that God was their King, and He established a system for the society to live by. The law was given through Moses and established God's desire for His people to be holy, as He is holy (Leviticus 19:2). These rules didn't impede their lives; in fact, it did the opposite. As they lived according to God's design and statutes, they could enjoy life to its fullest and serve God with all their heart, soul, mind, and strength (Deuteronomy 28:1-14). And if they disobeyed God, they would be overtaken with curses (Deuteronomy 28:15-68). The Israelites were given specific instructions about their lives, including their sexuality.

Virginity until the wedding night has always been God's standard. Newly married couples participated in a custom to prove the new bride's virginity. The Israelites would place a sheet on the couple's bed so that when they consummated their marriage, a sign of blood would reveal the young woman's virginity until their sexual intercourse that night.

The Lord created women with a hymen membrane that was meant to remain intact until the first sexual encounter. The blood would be a sign of the sealing of the covenant with her husband. Ultimately the sign was to point to the coming Savior, who would die for our sins on the cross. His blood would be poured out on the cross as a sign of His covenant with us, as Jesus said: "For this is my blood of the covenant, which is poured out for many for the forgiveness of sins" (Matthew 26:28).

The sheet that proved the young woman's virginity would be given to her father as a safeguard in case a false accusation of sexual fornication or sex before marriage was brought against her (Deuteronomy 22:13-21). After their marriage was consummated, the husband and wife would celebrate and enjoy each other by spending seven days together in a back room of the home of the young woman's family. Meanwhile, family and friends would be celebrating in the front of the home. After their seven-day honeymoon, the husband would present his wife. Then the married couple would celebrate with friends and family the beauty of their lifelong covenant.[7]

With such specific instructions and laws, the Israelites were also warned of specific consequences if those laws were broken. They knew that sexual sin could result in the death penalty by stoning. This punishment was administered not out of hate, but in order to purge the evil and corruption from Israel, helping the people to maintain a pure and upright society. God judged many crimes to be so wicked that they were worthy of death, including murder.

While murder causes the physical death of one's body, sexual immorality brings other kinds of death—the death of innocence, health, stability, fidelity, faithfulness, trust, joy, peace, and security. The pleasure and high of the moment deceitfully will lead a person to the slaughter. As James 1:15 says, "Then desire when it has conceived gives birth to sin, and sin when it is fully grown brings forth death."

God's story and His love for mankind continues to unfold in the New Testament. In John 8, a woman who had cheated on her husband was taken by the religious leaders to Jesus. They failed to bring the man who was also guilty and told Jesus about her sin of adultery. According to the law, her sentence would have been death. The crowd of men asked Jesus what His judgment was.

Jesus responded, "Let him who is without sin among you be the first to throw a stone at her" (John 8:7). He made it clear that only a person who had never sinned could uphold the law in that moment and administer the death penalty. After the crowd heard this, they started to leave, from the oldest to the youngest, because they realized they were all guilty of sin. After the entire crowd left, the woman remained in Jesus' presence.

> "Woman, where are they? Has no one condemned you?" Jesus asked her.
> The woman responded, "No one, Lord."
> Jesus replied, "Neither do I condemn you; go, and from now on sin no more." (John 8:10-11)

I was amazed. According to the law, Jesus had every right to give that woman the death penalty, but He didn't. Instead He gave her exactly what I had been given: His grace.

She had experienced the sorrow and consequences of sexual sin, but now she had found a beautiful hope. She found a promise that her life could be redeemed. And so, because of His great love, Jesus paid a heavy price for that woman's sins and for the sins of the world. In the same gospel of John, another event is recorded several chapters later—the crucifixion of Jesus Christ. In John 19, I read about Jesus being nailed to a cross. He hung from it with thick nails holding His body there.

Above His bleeding head, a sign was placed which read, "Jesus of Nazareth, the King of the Jews." He died on that cross later that afternoon (John 19:33). He received the death penalty for the sins of the world, even though He was innocent. Justice was issued—at God's expense—through the perfect, spotless sacrifice of His Son. The temple veil tore from top to bottom, signifying the access believers have to God's presence (Matthew 27:51). And after three days, Jesus trampled death and Satan's power by rising from the dead (John 20).

Determined to learn more about God's view of sex and purity, I came across another book at the bookstore titled *I Kissed Dating Goodbye* by Joshua Harris. His title puzzled me. *Why would this man give up on dating? Could there be dangers in dating?*

I purchased the book and eagerly turned page after page to understand his perspective. He explained the danger of individuals investing in a relationship outside the context, commitment, and sanctity of marriage because of the risk of defrauding one another or taking advantage of people and dishonoring God.

Josh described our culture's way of dating as a game. In this game, two people invest their time, emotions, and even their bodies to the relationship. When one person decides the other isn't meeting his needs or when someone else comes along who seems more attractive, the relationship can be broken off and each party moves on. Broken relationships cause broken hearts. God wants us to protect and cherish each other's heart and life, rather than using or abusing each other.

In his book, Josh explained that getting to know someone we're interested in should be done carefully. Protecting the person's heart and body should be our utmost priority, not lusting after them for selfish gain.

I set down Josh's book and determined that if I was interested in a man, I would accept his invitation and go on a date. I figured that after three casual dates of our getting to know each other, we would know if our values and life goals lined up. I would ask myself, *Is this a man I can follow? Is this a man I can serve?* While I understood that three dates couldn't be a set-in-stone kind of pattern for everyone, it helped me keep things casual with men and not let emotions and hopes get hyped up for me or for him. One man actually thanked me for my forthrightness. I knew that he, as my brother in Christ, deserved a clear yes or no. Trifling with a man's mind wasn't anything I wanted to do.

Purity also meant modesty. One friend explained to me that he "bounces" his eyes away from females who dress provocatively. And one male friend explained the importance of viewing females from their neck up. I understood that while men have the responsibility to exercise self-control, females can help by not wearing clothing that is tight or revealing. I heard that modesty isn't so much about covering our bodies as it is about revealing our dignity.

God's Word explains that our actions and words always flow out of our heart (Matthew 5:18). And what we meditate on becomes a pattern of thinking. I put away my secular music and started listening to Christian music, which had encouraging, uplifting lyrics. I stayed away from movies and places that didn't honor God, not in a legalistic way but out of a desire to keep my mind pure. As Scripture says, "Do not conform to the pattern of this world, but be transformed by the renewing of your mind. Then you will be able to test and approve what God's will is—his good, pleasing and perfect will" (Romans 12:2).

Through my studies, a picture was painted: God desires His people to be set apart as His pure bride, our purity is possible because of the grace we receive at the cross, and a lifestyle of purity is a direct result of God's enabling and empowerment. The way He has commanded us to live *is* possible!

I began this journey with simplicity and innocence; I didn't consider the possibility of facing the fire of sexual temptation. I never thought about how personal justifications can easily lead to the slippery slope of compromise. And while we may be able to convince ourselves that compromise is okay, Scripture says there shouldn't be even a hint of sexual immorality in our lives (Ephesians 5:3). Also, I didn't consider that my unwritten timeline of being married by age twenty-five or twenty-six might not match God's plan.

Reflection

- What are some things you've learned about purity? Why is a lifestyle of purity so important?

____

____

____

____

____

____

____

____

- What are some practical ways you can walk in purity? Ask God for strength and for faith to trust Him, even when it's hard.

____

____

____

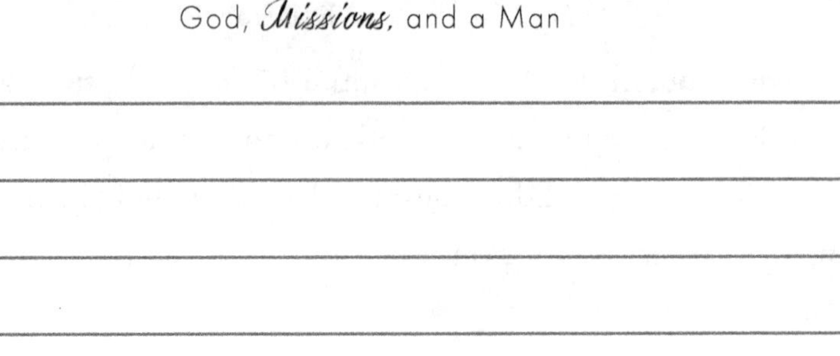

Meditation

For this is the will of God, your sanctification: that you abstain from sexual immorality (1 Thessalonians 4:3).

That no one transgress and defraud his brother in this matter, because the Lord is an avenger in all these things, as we told you beforehand and solemnly warned you (1 Thessalonians 4:6).

Treat younger men as brothers and younger women as sisters with absolute purity (1 Timothy 5:1-2).

Our redemption:

As far as the east is from the west, so far does he remove our transgressions from us (Psalm 103:12).

Therefore, if anyone is in Christ, he is a new creation. The old has passed away; behold, the new has come (2 Corinthians 5:17).

There is therefore now no condemnation for those who are in Christ Jesus (Romans 8:1).

Chapter Four

A Voodoo Village

The people who walked in darkness have seen a great light; those who dwelt in a land of deep darkness, on them has light shone.
(Isaiah 9:2)

We jolted around in our seats in the large yellow van as we traveled down a dirt road laden with massive potholes. I looked outside my dusty window. Women effortlessly balanced large baskets on their heads as they walked along a path that paralleled the road.

Suddenly Pastor Charles honked his horn and yelled something at another driver and made the turn. The rules of traffic seemed to be that whoever honked persistently and demanded their way, got the right of way.

I looked toward Kelly and grinned. She smiled back. *This is Africa.*

Traveling to Africa was a result of Kelly's leadership. One year earlier, as we sat on chairs in a youth group meeting, she explained to us a desire set deeply in her heart: "Ever since I was a little girl, my dream has been to go to Africa." Her eyes met ours. "In fact, I would love to take you girls to Africa!"

My heart leapt in my chest. Bringing the greatest message to another continent sounded intriguing. I caught her vision and went home that evening with the exciting news.

"Dad! Guess what?" I followed him as he made his way to another room. "Kelly wants to bring us to Africa!" My dad looked at me, probably to see if I was serious.

"Absolutely not!" he responded and shut the door in my face.

I understood. Allowing his teen daughter to go to a continent often known for its peril could place me in harm's way. I looked at the closed door in front of me, but I didn't let it shake my resolve.

We wasted no time and began to raise funds. My uncle donated his large vegetable garden, and in time my dad's heart took a turn. He ended up donating a field of hay bales to us. We were given the tasks of harvesting the vegetables and moving the bales from the field, and the profit was ours. After several months of fundraising, we had the amount we needed.

A couple of weeks after graduating from high school and running in the Minnesota state track meet, Kelly and I plus three other girls in the Bible study flew across the Atlantic Ocean and landed several hours later in Accra, Ghana.

As Pastor Charles drove us from the airport to his home, he welcomed us to his African country, known as the Gold Coast due to the abundance of gold discovered there by Europeans in the 1400s. "I am very happy that you have come to my home in Ghana to serve our Almighty God together." Pastor Charles spoke in impeccable English, which is the official language of Ghana. "The

Lord will bless you abundantly!" His charisma was contagious, and I looked forward to his leadership.

My excitement quickly faded into confusion when we turned down a street. The sun had just set, and scores of people were gathered on the roadside—they stretched out blankets and began to lie down. *Why are so many people preparing to sleep on the edge of the road?*

Pastor Charles broke the thick silence in the van. "Many people in Ghana move from their rural villages to the city looking for work," he explained. "Since it is very difficult to find work in the city, many people—including children—end up on the street without a home. When the rainy season comes…" He paused for a moment, "many children are swept away in the currents."

Swept away in the currents? Isn't there a safe place for the children to sleep? This would be the first of many sobering facts I would face in Africa.

After several minutes, we arrived at Pastor Charles' compound. We met his wife, Sophia, and crashed on mattresses underneath a ceiling fan that circulated the thick warm air.

The next morning, my eyes shot open to the coursing rhythm of a corn broom scraping the concrete outside our room. I jumped out of bed and tiptoed to the bathroom. A large bin of water stood next to the shower. I hopped into the shower, dipped a small bucket into the bin, and caught my breath as the cool water rushed over me.

After the bucket shower, I found the girls situating their belongings, and my bedmate had all her belongings strewn out across our mattress. I grinned as I watched her meticulously rearranging and organizing her belongings. I sat on the corner of the bed, and we joked about her swift commandeering of the bed.

After getting situated, we went to the dining room and found homemade bread, boiled eggs, and pineapple on the table. "Good morning, my angels," Pastor Charles said as he joined us in the dining room. He led us in prayer, and we began to eat. "Today," he said, "we are going to feed a village." We had raised funds for this endeavor, and our goal was to provide a hot meal to an entire village.

After breakfast, I ventured outside. Women were stirring massive metal pots containing gallons of orange rice and chicken on top of small fires. We loaded the large pots into the back of the van.

As we left the city, the dry and arid land became green and lush. Three hours later, we arrived at the village and parked on the roadside near some mud huts with thatched roofs. People from the village approached us. Many children had protruding abdomens and thin arms, yet they all donned smiles on their beautiful faces. Some women had almond-shaped scars on their cheeks that we learned later represented their tribal identity.

We set up the large pots ready to distribute the food, starting with the children. We worked fervently filling one Styrofoam container after another, until every person in the village had been fed. Afterward, we saw some children sitting with their Styrofoam container unopened. We asked why they weren't eating, and they explained that they were saving it to share with their entire family.

Pastor Charles had told us that we were only going to one village, but afterward he told us to load the van so we could go to a neighboring village. Once we arrived, we fed the people there as well. Since we still had food, he told us to load the van again, so we could travel to a third village.

We asked Pastor Charles how we were able to feed three villages. Pastor Charles shrugged his shoulders, "God multiplied the food. It happens sometimes." I was astonished. *What other miracles would we witness?*

We left the village and headed back to Accra. In our vehicle, I sat in the front, next to Pastor Charles. The streets of Accra were bustling with traffic and people.

"Look! There's a mahogany tree!" Pastor Charles exclaimed as he pointed to a massive tree with dark bark on the edge of the road. I grabbed my camera and took a picture of the tree.

"Hey, you!" A man on the street caught my attention. "I'm going to throw you in jail!" he shouted. He stood shirtless in front of a loaded cart that he set down. His eyes burning with anger, he thrust out his finger at me. I dropped my camera. My stomach sank. I never meant to expose him, and now I wanted to disappear.

"No, you are not going to throw her in jail!" Pastor Charles yelled back. "I am going to discipline you!" Pastor Charles unbuckled his belt and grabbed his door handle. The man spun back around. It was becoming clear that Pastor Charles was our shepherd *and* our protector.

The next morning after the broom alarm and bucket showers, Pastor Charles informed us that we would visit a school in Accra. Upon our arrival, hundreds of smiling faces peered out of large open windows of the school. Kelly split up our group, and she and I made our way to a fifth-grade classroom. We introduced ourselves to the teacher, and she introduced us to her class. I mentally counted fifty students. They peered at us with huge grins and looked as if they would explode with excitement.

"We are so happy to be with you today!" Kelly exclaimed. We taught a Bible lesson and helped the children memorize a verse.

They yelled out the verse and memorized it effortlessly. Then the kids started to move around like bees in a hive. I took out my camera and captured their joy and enthusiasm. Suddenly the teacher looked up and commanded her students to find their seats. In less than five seconds, all the children were seated in silence. Then one child spoke out of turn. She struck the child's hand with a long thin stick she carried. His face cringed, and he swiftly shook his hand up and down. The classroom was completely still. *Yikes! The children know to tow the line because of the swift repercussions.*

Kelly turned to me. "Okay, Kristine, share the gospel with them."

I looked back at her, but she'd already focused her attention back on the children. *But I've never preached the gospel before!* I tried to swallow my nerves without success. I breathed in deeply.

"God is our Creator, and He knows us and loves us deeply," I began. "But our sin separates us from Him and has eternal consequences." The little ones gazed back at me with their brown eyes as I spoke. "Jesus came to restore the relationship that was broken. If you turn from your sins and put your faith in Him, you will be saved." We closed our time together in prayer. I exhaled, relieved that the gospel was simple enough for an ordinary person to explain.

After an energy-infused hour of recess, we said goodbye to these joy-filled souls, and hopped into the mission van to go home.

"The freedom that's allowed to share about God is truly amazing," Kelly said earnestly on our ride home.

"Yes," Pastor Charles said. "We teach our children about God so they can become good people. But the United States is a Christian nation; surely they allow the same."

"No," Kelly replied sadly, as she looked out her window. "Public schools in the United States don't have the freedom to teach Christian values."

A few days later, Pastor Charles told us he wanted to take us to the village where he had grown up. We drove for several minutes. While still in Accra, when we stopped and exited the van, several children rushed toward us. I noticed immediately that their skin held a greyish tone, unlike the rich brown we had seen everywhere else. We took out our cameras to capture the silly poses Ghanaian children loved to strike. However, they didn't flock to the camera. Instead, one of the children began to grab for the others, urgently warning them. It seemed as if he believed one click would steal their souls.

We put away our cameras. Then the child who was rescuing the others went up to Kelly and spoke a few words with authority. He quickly motioned his arm up and then down. *Did he just cast a spell on her?* Kelly smiled and patted his head, but she looked just as disturbed as I felt. Pastor Charles walked ahead of us and didn't seem fazed by our surroundings. I tried to brush off the strange occurrence.

We followed Pastor Charles and walked farther into the village along a dirt road. A few Africans sat on the roadside vending food. They stared at us blankly. It looked like the village was having some kind of celebration, but there was no clear display of excitement or emotion. *Why are the kids terrorized by cameras? Why did a child try to put a spell on Kelly?*

Pastor Charles brought us to a white gate beside the road. We followed him into a courtyard. We squeezed together to fit in the small space. I peered over the shoulders of my teammates. A few African men were kneeling on the ground, and they were holding a ceramic bowl. The bowl had crushed corn in it, with a dead goat soaking in its blood.

At that moment, everything became clear. *We're in the middle of a voodoo ceremony!* I watched in disbelief, wondering what they would do with the carcass.

Pastor Charles conversed with the man holding the bowl, who smiled and waved at us. We waved back.

After a few minutes, Pastor Charles motioned for us to exit the courtyard. *Yes! Let's go before something even more bizarre occurs!*

It seemed that these rituals were commonplace for Pastor Charles, but they were unnatural to us. And sadly, the fear and heavy oppression that resulted from calling on evil was evident everywhere, even among the children. Pastor Charles explained to us later that he was friends with the voodoo priest in the village, and that his mission was to see him and his village saved. He explained that he and the Christian men he discipled had shared the Word of God with the villagers and hoped to see salvation soon.

At another village that practiced voodoo, we saw one little girl with dreadlocks in her jet-black hair. One of our translators told us that she'd been dedicated to the demons. Her parents had lost two of their children during labor, so they promised to give their next child to the spirits, if she lived. A few of us went up to her and placed our hands on her head. She looked into my eyes, but her face failed to show any light. Silently, we prayed for her soul and her protection from any evil. In the same village, we learned that babies are sacrificed to the spirits to obtain favor. *Why are the innocent handed over to evil?*

We had raised funds for a well for this village and had wired the funds to Pastor Charles before our arrival to Africa. We unveiled the well which would provide clean water for the entire village. They were given clean water that would provide health and well-being, yet it was evident that their souls needed *living* water. Pastor Charles preached about water that was not from a well—water that they could drink and never thirst again (John 4).

One morning I woke up and felt the heat of a fever rush over my body. I told myself, *Just get ready, like everyone else*. Kelly must have noticed that I looked ill. She reached over and felt my forehead.

"You're burning up," she said. She determined that I should stay home for the day. I lay back down, disappointed that I would miss out on the mission that day.

Before long, Pastor Charles entered our domain. His eyes communicated clearly his concern. "My angel is sick," he said. He placed his hand on my head and then my feet, and said, "In the name of Jesus Christ, heal Kristine from her head to her toes." The next morning the fever broke (James 5:16).

On Sunday we climbed the stairs of a pink concrete building adjacent to their home. Rows of plastic chairs filled the room, and the church was nearly packed. We found some seats near the front. Vibrant threads of fabric were woven in the women's dresses, some of which I recognized from my research as *kente* cloth, which had been the cloth worn by kings.

Large speakers reverberated as men beat congas and strummed guitars. The Africans jumped in rhythm and swayed their arms in the air. Pastor Charles encouraged us to join the celebration. We eagerly joined the others at the front and laughed as we tried to follow their God-given rhythm.

After a while, I made my way back to my chair next to an elderly woman. Suddenly, as if she couldn't sit any longer, she rose from her seat. In her hunched-over stance, she began shuffling to the rhythm.

Tears welled up in my eyes as I witnessed her beautiful praise. I was seeing two vastly different cultures come together in one accord to worship our risen King. There was no clock in the church, and time was swept away by the praises of the Africans.

After our lengthy time of worship in song, Pastor Charles preached passionately on the importance of being a vessel of God's love and truth to a desperate world.

After serving with Pastor Charles for two and a half weeks, our time in Africa came to an end. For the last time, we hopped into the yellow mission van. Several Africans joined us on our journey to the airport. A sad melody filled the van as our African friends sang. I didn't understand the words, but I understood the song's message. Looking out the window, tears filled my eyes as I said goodbye to those who had shown me what it meant to live and give Christ my all (Philippians 3:14).

Reflection

- Do you have a mentor in your life who challenges you to go outside your comfort zone? Can you explain some ways that he or she has done this?

____

____

____

____

- Do you have godly examples in your life who live out the gospel of Jesus? How have they demonstrated their faith?

Meditation

Remember your leaders, those who spoke to you the word of God. Consider the outcome of their way of life, and imitate their faith (Hebrews 13:7).

Declare his glory among the nations, his marvelous works among all the people (Psalm 96:3).

And he sat down and called the twelve. And he said to them, "If anyone would be first, he must be last of all and servant of all" (Mark 9:35).

Chapter Five
Joy, Pain, and Praise

Don't forget in the darkness what you have learned in the light.
(Joseph Bayly)

Their smiles radiated off the computer screen as I clicked through my photos. Mud huts in the background and their protruding abdomens screamed of their colossal challenges.

I wanted to return to Africa equipped as a nurse. However, shortly before graduating from high school, my first choice in colleges, Prairie Bible Institute, informed me that their nursing program was full. I settled on my second choice, a college close to home, and a program of Intercultural Studies. My plans were set. However, one week before the first day of fall semester, I received an unexpected phone call.

"Hi, Kristine. My name is Candace, and I'm the admissions

director at Prairie Bible College," the lady on the line said enthusiastically.

"Hi," I said. *Why is Prairie calling me?* The last call informed me that the program of my choice was maxed out.

"Someone dropped out of the nursing program," she explained, "and a spot opened up. Are you interested in attending?"

My mind bounced back and forth between the two colleges but snapped back to reply. "Yes, I'm interested." I hesitated. "Can I call you back with an answer?"

"Yes, of course," she responded.

We hung up, and without time to process, I explained the phone call to my parents. "What do you think I should do?" I asked them. My eyes felt wide, wondering what all this could mean.

"I think you should get Pastor Steve's advice," my dad responded.

Pastor Steve was the youth pastor at Woodland Bible Church. *Yes! That's a great idea!* I dialed the church phone number, and Pastor Steve answered.

"Hi, Pastor Steve," I began. "I was wondering if my dad and I could come to your office to get some advice about college." He quickly agreed to my request, and we were there within minutes.

In his office, Pastor Steve greeted us with a smile. "Please sit down," he invited.

After I explained my strange twist of events and scattered thoughts, he nodded. "The thing is," he began, "Prairie Bible College is world-renowned for missions." His eyes began to glisten as he spoke. "If you want to be a missionary, go to Prairie Bible College."

My racing thoughts froze.

I simply stared at the pastor. Nothing had changed in the room, but the power of his words had. I knew that God was speaking through him. All at once, I knew what to do.

"Thank you, Pastor Steve." I flew out of his office, sure of my direction.

A few days later, we crossed the Canadian border and merged onto the Trans-Canada Highway, which extends for thousands of miles across the entire country. I sat in the back seat of my parents' car. After several hours, I peered outside the vehicle's window at the treeless, desolate land. Our journey and the highway seemed endless. *It's so far from home*, I thought anxiously. *I'm not sure I want to do this anymore!* For a moment I panicked. It was all I could do from shouting out, "Turn around, I don't want to go to college there!" If I had opened my mouth and spoken those words of panic, I knew that my dad wouldn't have hesitated to turn around and bring me home. But I kept silent. We continued the journey on the never-ending highway.

Our travels seemed endless, but after eighteen hours we finally arrived at the campus in the farming community of Three Hills, Alberta. The campus was quaint and quiet. In the dorms, only a few girls were getting their belongings situated into their rooms. I figured more would be coming throughout the weekend. I got settled into my room, and it was time to say goodbye to my parents.

As we stood in the parking lot, my mom's eyes were glazed over, but a smile broke through. I held on to the used bike my parents had picked up for me earlier that weekend. I was stoked to have a solid mode of transportation.

"Well, I guess this is goodbye," I said, with a sliver of doubt still lingering in my mind. The campus and the dorms felt empty and unfamiliar. I didn't have anyone to call friend, and the campus didn't feel like home. I didn't want my parents to worry, so I didn't let them in on my uncertainty.

"We're only a phone call away," my dad said, as my mom nodded. "Call us anytime for anything." I thought I could see tears welling up in my dad's eyes but couldn't be sure.

We embraced in the small parking lot next to the admissions building. And there, my parents made a brave decision. They didn't try to put a halt on my potentially dangerous dreams; instead, they gave me over to the Lord and trusted His plan for my life. I couldn't fully understand the weight of this reality, but because of their blessing, I was given the opportunity to give Jesus my all.

After embracing my parents, they jumped into their car. I hopped on my turquoise bike and rode across the college campus. As the summer Canadian air swept across my face, I sensed an unmistakable assurance deep in my heart that could come only from a good and loving Father. "But now, O Lord, you are our Father" (Isaiah 64:8a).

The next day, I stood in the college admissions building, waiting in line to sign up for my nursing and Bible classes. A girl my age was in line as well. She turned around and introduced herself.

"I'm Hannah from Montana, and I'm in the nursing program," she said. Her Montana accent was just as fun as her outgoing, friendly personality.

"You have a bike?" she exclaimed after introductions. "I have a bike too! You know, I heard that the three hills are *that* way." She pointed with an outstretched arm.

We plotted to find these mysterious three hills. After signing up for classes, Hannah and I grabbed our bikes and pedaled away from campus. We glided down a hill toward the edge of the town and found ourselves on a gravel road surrounded by fields of golden wheat. We breathed in the fresh air, and after several minutes, we could see the massive hills. After a few more miles, we arrived at the foot of one of the hills.

We lowered gears and began the steep trek, pressing against the incline. My legs started to burn halfway up as we pushed toward our goal. I gulped in the prairie air and looked ahead at Hannah. I already loved her keen sense of adventure.

Finally, we reached the summit. We stood clasping our bikes on top of the world and gazed at the unending rolling prairie as we caught our breath. The sun had begun its descent and radiated off the glistening fields. We took in the spectacular view and talked about God's incredible creation. Then we took our bikes and cascaded down the gravel road, allowing the steep slope to dictate our velocity. Hannah flew ahead of me, and we drank in every ounce of adrenaline the momentum provided.

As the weekend progressed, the campus buzzed with students ready to prepare for pastoral responsibilities, athletic coordination, and youth pastoral roles. The college was filled with like-minded individuals, and this camaraderie allowed for flourishing friendships throughout the semester.

When we weren't immersed in our studies, we delved into adventures around the small town and reveled in the beauty of living in a community of believers. In the girls' dorms, we often lay sprawled out for hours as we talked about God, life, and the desires of our hearts. We spurred each other on to follow Jesus more passionately and to live lives of purity.

"Females are emotionally wired," a friend explained one day as we hung out in her dorm room. "And when we share our feelings or deep things of our heart, we become attached to the male on an emotional level. This attachment is meant only for our future husbands, since it's part of the bonding process of a husband and a wife becoming one flesh."

Another friend told me, "A girl's heart should be so lost in God that the man has to go to Him to find her."

I learned that purity is not just physical in nature; it also involves the deep affections of the heart. I decided that except for my family and friends, only my future husband would hear these three words from me: *I love you.* Those words would be a verbal sign for my future husband to know that he would have all my heart and affections. "I adjure you, O daughters of Jerusalem, that you not stir up or awaken love until it pleases" (Song of Solomon 8:4).

After two adventurous and intensive years at Prairie, this joy-filled journey—like many great adventures—came to an end. My time at Prairie helped establish my faith. I gained skills as a licensed practical nurse, and I was ready to return to Africa.

My final course was a nursing practicum. With a number of hospitals and environments to choose from, several other nursing students and I opted for Mozambique in southeast Africa. Suzanne, one of our nursing instructors—and the most compassionate and competent nurse I knew—would be our leader.

After a string of endless flights across Canada, the Atlantic Ocean, and the massive African continent, we landed in Beira, Mozambique, along with several other classmates. After deboarding, we were met by Rick, the missionary who would host us. I was relieved to be warmly welcomed by our host and to hop into a van instead of another plane.

As we settled into the van, suddenly my body felt bone-weary, and my mind seemed foggy. I closed my eyes, and the team and I were in and out of sleep as we made our way to our destination in the bush.

Hours later I felt the van jolt, and I opened my heavy eyelids. Several mud huts were clustered together on the side of the highway. We turned down a gravel road and passed by the huts. At the end of the gravel road, a cluster of tents had been pitched. We had finally arrived. Five small tents would be our living quarters for the month. Our host explained that there was a path through the trees behind our tents that led to a river and waterfall that we could check out anytime.

After unloading the van, we were assigned tentmates. Heidi, a dear friend full of joy and mischief, would be my tentmate. I unzipped our tent to reveal two small cots on either side of the two-person tent. We quickly zipped it back up to prevent mosquitoes from entering. As we got settled into our living quarters, the sun set, and darkness descended over the land.

Heidi and I swapped lighthearted bedtime stories. Then, just as I was on the verge of slumber, the eerie sound of rhythmic drums echoed from across the river. The thick darkness was suddenly tangible. *Voodoo drums.* I tried to imagine what the nocturnal ceremony across the river entailed, and I wondered if we would ever encounter peril from our neighbors. My heart began pounding in sync with the pulsating rhythm as I faded into a deep sleep.

The next morning, Suzanne briefed us on our tasks. Using lessons we'd prepared in Canada, we would teach schoolchildren effective hygienic practices. We jumped into the van to drive to the school. On our arrival, dozens of children swarmed our van to greet their foreign visitors.

As the school day commenced, we taught the children in the concrete school structure how to effectively clean their teeth with a stick and to rinse their mouth with water after eating anything sweet. After teaching the children about hygiene, I took out some laminated coloring sheets from my backpack. The sheets portrayed Jesus on the cross. I asked the children if they knew who this man was on the cross. With wonder in their eyes, some of the children said, "Jay-zus." *Maybe they go to a Christian church.*

After we taught the children, hundreds of women with their babies lined up outside the classroom for immunizations. Suzanne explained that word must have spread to the surrounding villages about our free vaccinations. The line wrapped around the school to a veranda where we prepared to give the injections. I wrapped my fingers in medical tape and donned gloves. Through our translator, I instructed moms to secure their infants, as I viewed anatomical markers before the injection. We assessed and immunized hundreds of babies.

At the end of the week, Heidi and I were assigned to work in a clinic. The two-room clinic stood on the other side of the gravel road leading to our commune. At the clinic, we assessed, diagnosed, and treated our patients, who ranged from newborn infants to the elderly.

Several parents brought their toddlers in with second-degree burns. We learned that while these little ones were learning to walk, they had tripped and stumbled into an open cooking fire. As we gently cleansed their wounds, tears streamed down their faces. Their eyes were full of pain and uncertainty, and my heart broke over their anguish. Other children were brought in with circular burn marks from playing a game of grabbing sticks from a fire and jabbing their companions. We instructed the families to return after a few days so we could change the wound dressings.

One day Suzanne explained to us that an elderly man in a neighboring village had fallen and sustained a broken hip. Fred had been admitted to the provincial hospital in Beira, and Suzanne assigned a few others and me to help transport him back home.

When we arrived at the large hospital and walked through the entrance, a foul smell filled the air. A thin line of brown fluid marked the tiled hallway. Nausea swept over me as we pushed past the alarming smell and fluid. When we found Fred's room, we saw seven other patients on cots crammed into the small room. One boy had an external fixation device on his leg, and his dad was next to him. I smiled at him and hoped beyond hope that he was receiving the care he needed. *This must be the orthopedic unit.*

Suzanne viewed the x-ray and confirmed her suspicions. "He has four fractures on his hip," she said, as she traced the darker lines on the x-ray.

One of the nurses abruptly responded, "No fractures—just dislocated!"

We didn't argue with this nurse. Instead, we palpated and assessed the large plaster cast from Fred's hip to his toes. We noted that the cast prevented Fred from bending his leg, but it failed to restrain movement of his hip. *Why don't these healthcare workers know how to properly construct a cast? Why don't they know how to interpret an x-ray?* I imagined standing outside the hospital and warning everyone to turn around and go receive care elsewhere.

Interrupting my thoughts, a nurse began to shout out commands toward Fred. Despite the language barrier, obviously she had ordered Fred to move from the hospital bed to the gurney. Fred began to sit up and move.

"No," Suzanne intervened. "We'll help him."

Taking over, my team and I properly splinted Fred's leg with sticks and blankets and planned on removing the useless cast later. We wheeled him out of this hospital from hell and gave him a Tylenol 3 to relieve his pain.

We loaded Fred into the back of our pickup truck, and Hannah joined him. Through the window between the bed and cab, I heard her praying. After a while she said, "Amen." After a slight pause, we heard Fred say, "One prayer will cover me for a while, but please pray for me more." So, Hannah continued to pray with Fred. I saw that Fred believed in praying without ceasing (1 Thessalonians 5:17).

On our way to his village, Suzanne and I constructed a care plan for his family to implement. The goal was to promote healing and to prevent pneumonia.

When we arrived at his village, we parked next to a small concrete structure. His family welcomed us and helped us prepare his room, which was small, with little air circulation. A thin mat was stretched on the floor.

We carried Fred into the room using a blanket as a stretcher. Ensuring that his hip was immobile, we lowered him onto the mat. Next, Suzanne and I explained the care plan to his wife, leaving Fred in his room to rest.

A few days later, we went to visit Fred. Suzanne explained to us that he had developed pneumonia. She asked if I wanted to talk with Fred. We went into his room. Fred was in the same place where we had placed him. I knelt down and held Fred's hand while I put my other hand on his chest. The coarse rumbling of fluid in his lungs rattled against my palm.

"Fred, it's okay," I said, looking into his eyes.

He asked us to pray for him. We prayed with Fred and read from John 14:

> "Let not your hearts be troubled. Believe in God; believe also in me. In my Father's house are many rooms. If it were not so, would I have told you that I go to prepare a place for you? And if I go and prepare a place for you, I will come again and will take you to myself, that where I am you may be also." (vv. 1-3)

After we prayed with Fred, we left and drove back to our camp. Later that evening, Suzanne called a brief meeting around the evening fire with the team. We met there every evening throughout the week to process our day. She informed us that Fred had passed away.

I stared at the flames. I didn't want to believe it. We all knew that he had passed away not in a comfortable bed surrounded by medical amenities; rather, he had slipped into eternity on a small mat, breathing stale air, and with only meager means to relieve his discomfort. Tears filled my eyes. We knew that his passing was painful, but we also knew that whatever suffering he experienced was relieved now in the presence of Jesus. We ended our meeting with prayer, lifting up the beautiful people of Africa who are plagued with unthinkable ailments.

As we continued to serve, we saw that HIV/AIDS, tuberculosis, malaria, poverty, and malnutrition had infiltrated the people. Spending one month to relieve their suffering seemed equivalent to placing a drop in the ocean. But perhaps, as Mother Theresa had said, "We know only too well that what we are doing is nothing more than a drop in the ocean. But if the drop were not there, the ocean would be missing something."

Several times we parked the van on the side of the road to meet with a particular mom in order to treat her malnourished baby. She had a two-month-old daughter who looked like a premature newborn. We put her on the scale; her weight was 5.5 pounds. Her arms were thin and her skin frail. The mom explained that her baby wasn't taking her breast milk.

The mother's eyes reverberated with hope that we would save her little girl. We prayed for healing, and we met with the mom every day to help her malnourished baby gain strength and thrive. We tried feeding her milk through a syringe, and Suzanne started an IV through a tiny vein in her arm. But the baby did not get better. Days later, a blood test confirmed the presence of HIV. Like so many babies diagnosed with HIV/AIDS, she passed away long before her first birthday.

I didn't understand why the Lord didn't allow this child to be healed. After debriefing, I walked through the forest to the river and waterfalls, and I wept. I wept for the baby who died and for Fred. I wept for the child we saw earlier in the week who suffered in the heat of her hut with body aches and a high fever brought on by malaria. I wept for the healthcare facility in Beira that was failing to provide the care the Africans desperately needed. I wept for the village with the chief who had a deadly STI—the disease had taken over his entire body, and he admitted to sexual relations with countless women in his village.

If we were here to help people get better, why were people suffering and dying right before us? I cried out to the Lord in the darkness: "Lord," I said through my tears, "why all this suffering and death?"

Silence.

I needed an answer—a reason for all this misery. One of the girls on the team had posed the question of a God-forsaken land.

"Have You forsaken the Africans?" I asked.

Suddenly, through the tree branches above my station, sparks of light peeked through. It wasn't a cluster of stars—it was stars banded together in the unmistakable shape of a cross.

The Southern Cross is a constellation shining brightly in the sky of the southern hemisphere. I had seen it before but wasn't looking for it that night. Immediately I imagined Jesus dying on the cross for me and for all mankind—including the Africans.

No, You have not forsaken the Africans. I continued looking at the clear stellar image beaming through the branches. *You love the Africans so much that You sent Your Son to die for them, and You send a reminder every night of Your great love.*

My heart found its resolve. God had *not* forsaken the Africans. He had proven His great love on the cross, and He cares immensely for each and every person (John 3:16).

Every Sunday in Mozambique, we attended a Christian church down the road from us. We clapped our hands as songs rang out in another tongue, praising and lifting high the great I Am. Their voices were soaked with passion and conviction. Men beat congas as women danced with sleeping babies anchored to their backs. Children bounced up and down with their natural God-given rhythm. These people who cry out to Jesus seemed to understand His great love and unfailing presence, even in their suffering. It seemed that the Africans did not forget in the darkness what they had learned in the light.

Even amid this vibrancy of those who know Christ, voodoo is widely practiced by others. In the cool nights, as voodoo drums sounded, a thick and eerie spiritual presence crept over the land. On one occasion the darkness came especially near our camp. As we slept in our tents, just down the road Suzanne and Rick had a dangerous encounter with a demon-possessed man. Inside the man's thatched-roof hut, he shimmied up a fifteen-foot pole to its peak. Then he let go and fell into a fire. They rolled him out of the fire, and his intent became to harm Suzanne. He turned toward her and repeated again and again in the local dialect: "Kill, kill, kill." His friends eventually came and detained him. We learned later from Rick that this man was eventually freed from demonic possession, and that he accepted Christ as his Savior.

Although the darkness was evident, so was God's love and glory. Alongside the Southern Cross, we observed countless stars populate and light up the heavens. In a radiance that far surpasses the sky in North America, their vast number and splendor seemed to parallel the Africans' song and dance. We spent many nights with our eyes transfixed upward as we held on to our water bottles filled with hot water—the days were hot and humid, but the nights were chilly. These galactic views pointed to the greatness of our God. We prayed that the Africans would look up at the sky and know their Creator's great love. As Psalm 147:4 declares, "He determines the number of the stars; he gives to all of them their names."

After four rigorous weeks, we completed our nursing practicum. We left the astonishing continent of Africa, but we would not forget. We would remember their strength and faith even amid hardships. We would remember that Jesus' all-surpassing love reaches every corner of the earth. And even in the midst of pain, Jesus is there.

Reflection

- What do you think the purpose of pain is? How have you seen God's hand in the midst of your suffering? How have you seen His love?

- Is it possible to have joy and praise God in the midst of deep suffering? If so, how?

Meditation

Count it all joy, my brothers, when you meet trials of various kinds, for you know that the testing of your faith produces steadfastness. And let steadfastness have its full effect, that you may be perfect and complete, lacking in nothing (James 1:2-4).

In this you rejoice, though now for a little while, if necessary, you have been grieved by various trials, so that the tested genuineness of your faith—more precious than gold that perishes though it is tested by fire—may be found to result in praise and glory and honor at the revelation of Jesus Christ (1 Peter 1:6-7).

And do not be grieved, for the joy of the Lord is your strength (Nehemiah 8:10b).

Chapter Six

Underneath a Mango Tree

So Abraham called the name of that place,
"The Lord will provide."
(Genesis 22:14a)

Pass. Relief rushed over me to see that word on my computer screen—I had passed the national licensing exam for practical nurses (NCLEX-LPN). *Thank You, Lord!*

I moved back home and worked fervently to pay off my student loans. Debt wouldn't hold me back from serving, so I worked two jobs for several months until the balance dwindled to zero. I was twenty-two years old and ready for the next adventure.

I relocated to Minneapolis to a condo sponsored by my employer, Bayada. I continued to work as a pediatric home health nurse. One evening during a shift-change, a co-worker and sister in Christ relayed some surprising information.

"Hi, Kristine!" she exclaimed.

"Hi, Angela!" I replied, holding on to my white mocha, ready for the overnight shift.

In the dimly lit living room, the ventilator's soft and rhythmic sound faithfully administered twelve breaths a minute into the little girl's tracheostomy. I looked over Angela's shoulder to see that she was already sleeping soundly. The blue iridescent light of the vital signs monitor lit up her heart rate and oxygen saturation level.

I was amazed that this little girl had gone through so much, yet she always maintained her joyful and vibrant spirit. During the day, she didn't let any of the tubes get in her way as she navigated around the living room. With her diagnosis of ventricular septal defect, the plan was for her to undergo open-heart surgery once she gained enough weight.

After a change-of-shift report, Angela's eyes seemed to glow as she stated, "Did you know that Bayada is sponsoring nurses to serve in Haiti? You only have to commit to four weeks, and they'll pay for everything!"

I was shocked. *Bayada would actually send me overseas?* A year earlier, news reports had poured in following the catastrophic earthquake that had brought utter devastation in this already impoverished nation. Amid the desperation, looters and machete-wielding gangs rose up to lay claim to the scarce supply of food and water. I imagined helping to relieve the people's continued suffering, and I knew in that moment that if God opened the door, I would go.

The next day, I emailed Bayada and applied to serve. I told Mary Joe, a co-worker and friend, about the exciting opportunity. She also lived in the condo, and her vibrant, upbeat personality kept things interesting in Minneapolis. We became good friends despite our disparity in years. She convinced me that age is just a number.

Two months later, we found ourselves in the back of a caged truck. I looked at Mary Joe as I held on to a bar on top of the truck to keep my balance. *What a trooper she is!* Mary Joe was sitting on the bench lining the back of the truck.

A potent smell of diesel fuel and sewage suddenly flooded my nostrils. I looked outside our caged environment. The sun beat down mercilessly on the land and on people selling piles of vegetables along the roadside. They didn't seem bothered by the surprising smell or heat. I breathed in the thick humid air—a stark contrast to the dry winter air back home. We zoomed around pedestrians, motorcyclists, and vendors. *Aren't there any traffic laws here?*

Suddenly we passed a massive pile of concrete rubble. My mind shot back to the news on television about the 2010 earthquake. Reporters had filmed people digging desperately through mounds of debris trying to rescue victims trapped underneath. The desperation on their faces was haunting as they drudged and worked without equipment. Piles of rubble lay stagnant on the side of the road as a permanent burial ground for those unable to escape. I shuddered at the thought of those who never made it out.

We passed by blue tents perched on the edge of the road. I looked ahead and saw a sea of more blue tents. *Why are so many people still displaced?*

After several minutes, we stopped next to a high wall with razor wire stretched on top. A large gate opened, and an older Haitian man greeted us with a partially toothless grin.

Large tropical trees filled a courtyard that the roundabout enclosed. We circled around to park in front. As we parked, a Caucasian man wearing a button-up collared shirt and khaki cargo pants came out the front door. He had a cell phone clipped to his belt. He looked ready for any adventure, as if he'd just stepped off the set of *Indiana Jones.*

"Hello!" he said, beaming with enthusiasm. "Welcome to Haiti!" He grabbed our suitcases, and we followed him up the stairs into the Heart to Heart headquarters.

"I'm Dr. Spaulding," he said, as we made our way inside. "I'm the medical director of Heart to Heart International. It's a pleasure to have you here in Haiti—it must be cold this time of year in Minnesota!"

We learned that Dr. Spaulding was a retired medical internist. I was amazed that instead of living a comfortable and safe life in the United States, he chose to live and serve in a developing nation. Moreover, we found out later that his services were on a 100-percent voluntary basis.

After we placed our suitcases in our living quarters, Dr. Spaulding gave orientation right on the spot. We learned that Heart to Heart provides healthcare services through clinics in Port-au-Prince, Léogâne, and a remote region called Cascade Pétion. Dr. Spaulding told Mary Joe and me that in the morning we would be making the twelve-mile trek to Léogâne to serve at the clinic in the compound and to set up mobile clinics in the area. From the Heart to Heart base in Léogâne, we would travel to churches in the community and set up the clinics. He informed us that our journey to Léogâne would take about an hour because of traffic and road conditions.

"You know," Dr. Spaulding said in a heartfelt tone as he wrapped up our orientation, "the Haitians truly are remarkable people. One year ago, Heart to Heart responded immediately to the devastating earthquake. We didn't have sleeping quarters, so we slept outside. It was just days after the earthquake, and a group of people passed by us as we lay underneath the stars. They were singing 'Amazing Grace' as they walked by us."

He continued, "We knew the turmoil that their lives were bombarded with, and to hear them praising God was a great wonder." His eyes sparkled as he shared the story. "We're serving a resilient people whose faith can move mountains."

Dr. Spaulding's love and dedication to the Haitians was unmistakable. I looked forward to serving this resilient population and to be overseen by a medical director who I presumed would move mountains for them.

The next morning, we jumped into the caged truck. As we drove, I stood holding on to the top metal bar of the caged truck to take in our surroundings. Scores of people swarmed the streets. They looked like they were on a mission—going to work or to school. Children wore brightly colored uniforms with matching ribbons in their black and curly hair. Several people wore business attire. One lady, wearing a white dress, hopped into the local transportation called the Taptap, which was a pickup with a covered cab. Dr. Spaulding informed us that people tap the top or side of the pickup when they were ready to be dropped off. I wondered how the lady would keep her dress white all day.

After about an hour of being jolted around and being bombarded with an array of strong scents, we arrived at the compound in Léogâne. A fence surrounded the entire compound with razor wire on top. I was told later that before any building was constructed in Haiti, a wall was erected first to protect the property. A young Haitian man opened the gate to let us in, revealing a small house and a large cargo container that I assumed was the clinic. Mary Joe and I were introduced to Wilfred and Innocent, the two young men who would be our translators.

Dr. Spaulding had informed us that we would assess and triage patients before they would see the doctor and pharmacist. We would also help the pharmacist as needed.

I counted thirty people already waiting to be seen. The heat was starting to settle in, and the people were sitting on long benches underneath a massive mango tree in the front yard. Wilfrid gave instructions on what to expect.

After Wilfrid finished, I was put in the triage area right outside the container, while Mary Joe was placed in the pharmacy. Wilfrid translated my medical questions. As I began working, I noticed that many people wore dresses or other formal clothing. Dr. Spaulding had informed us in our orientation that people in Haiti came to a clinic wearing their best. I didn't understand why these people—who have so little and were not feeling well—would come looking their best. As they sat down on the chair to be assessed, they would light up and greet me with a smile.

A middle-aged woman sat down next to me, and I wrapped the blood pressure cuff around her arm.

"Wilfrid, can you ask her what brings her to the clinic today?" I asked.

After she answered, Wilfrid told me, "She says she was up all night last night shoveling water from her tent that came in from the storm. Her shoulder is hurting."

Shoveling water from her tent? She held onto her left shoulder and winced in pain. I stopped for a moment and looked into her eyes. I swallowed back my tears unsure I would be successful. I considered stepping aside for a few moments to regroup my feelings. *No,* I thought. *Be strong; serve her with the strength she's showing me.* I breathed in deeply and recorded her vitals and chief complaint.

"Mèsi," I said, and handed her the paper to give to the doctor.

The next morning, before our clinic started, I noticed a young boy standing by the front gate of our compound, peering in at the activities inside. He was maybe eight or nine years old and looked curious. I stepped out to greet him. His skin and eyes were a dark shade of brown.

Using the few Haitian Creole words that Wilfrid had taught me, I said, *"Bonjou! Kijan ou rele?"* (Good morning! What is your name?)

"Joseph," he answered in a thick Haitian accent.

I spoke slowly to make sure I was understood: *"Mwen rele Kristine."* (My name is Kristine.)

"Siret," he said.

I had no idea what that meant.

"Sooret?" I responded.

He nodded and motioned his hand up to his mouth.

"Just wait right there," I said. "I'll be right back!"

His eyes widened as he shook his head. I rushed back inside and asked Wilfrid what *sooret* meant, explaining that Joseph had put his hand to his mouth when he said it.

"Oh, *siret*," Wilfrid said. "That's candy."

I grabbed a couple of small lollipops from my duffel bag and went back to the gate. His face lit up, and he unwrapped the lollipop. I wanted to learn more about him, so I asked Wilfrid to help me.

Wilfrid came out to the gate with me. "Can you ask where his mom and dad are?"

My message was translated, and Joseph responded: *"Manman mwen te mouri. Papa'm rete nan Santo Domingo."*

Wilfrid explained that his mom was dead, and his dad lived in Santo Domingo. *Is he an orphan? Who does he live with? Why is his dad in Santo Domingo?* I asked who he was living with, and Wilfrid translated his response: "He lives down the street with his grandmother."

After our conversation, Joseph left, but he came to the compound again the next day, this time with friends.

"Siret," he said to me. His grinning cronies stood next to him.

I went back into the home, smiling as well. Word had spread that a *blan* (foreign) girl was handing out candy. I grabbed some lollipops for him and his buddies. The following week, a larger group of children congregated at the entrance of the compound. *Oh boy.* I thought looking at the motorcycles driving by. *The clan is stretching out into the street.*

It was endearing to me that these children came to visit at the gate, but I wondered if it would be possible to bring them inside to a safer environment. Then I could teach them about the One who loves them most. I asked the home manager if it would be possible to have the kids come in for a couple of hours every day after clinic. He hesitated and explained that the area was designated for patients and for Heart to Heart workers and volunteers—but after laying down a few stipulations, he agreed.

The next day, in the few Haitian words I knew, I welcomed the children into the compound. More than a dozen children flooded through the front gate. They jumped up and down, and I joined them in their celebration.

They sat down in chairs underneath the mango tree. I looked at their eager faces. *How am I going to share biblical truths with them?* Heart to Heart had translators, but they were paid workers and left after each clinic. I wasn't sure how to overcome the language barrier, so I prayed that God would help me learn their language.

The children came every day until we went back to Port-au-Prince for the weekend.

The following week, my children stormed into the compound, and they were followed by a teenage boy. I walked over to let him know that our Bible school was for younger children.

However, he spoke first and his words shocked me: "Hi, my name is Sonson."

He knew English!

"Hi, I'm Kristine," I responded.

"My full name is Saint Fordson Louis. And in Haiti," he explained, "if you have *son* at the end of your name, you can be called Sonson." He smiled confidently. He informed me that he could speak Creole, French, English, and Spanish. I was shocked. *How does he know four languages?*

Sonson also said, "I care about these children. They told me about you, and I wanted to come and meet you."

"Sonson, I want to teach them about Jesus," I explained, "but I don't speak Haitian Creole."

"I can help you with that," he replied. The Lord had provided a translator—and the language barrier had been shattered!

Sonson and I gathered the children underneath the mango tree and opened a children's Bible I had brought from home. The children were wide-eyed as I shared about Jonah, while Sonson translated. We asked them questions afterward, and they eagerly participated. Just as we finished, they kicked around a soccer ball.

Every day after clinic I looked forward to my children and Sonson arriving for the Bible lessons and fun. I gave Sonson a small wage for his assistance, so it became his after-school job.

"Kristine, I'm a believer in Jesus too," Sonson explained one day after the lesson. "I want to tell you how I became a Christian." He continued, "My mom was Catholic and always brought me to the Catholic church." Then he told me about the day in January 2010 when the huge earthquake struck. "I was inside our home studying, when my mom sent me on an errand. I had to walk far, but I didn't arrive because the earthquake hit. I ran back home and saw that our home had collapsed. If I had been inside, I would have died! Then a friend invited me to his Protestant church. When I went, I saw many differences, and I accepted Jesus."

I was amazed that beauty came out of the ashes. I looked around at the other children and wondered where each child was on that day when the ground convulsed underneath them.

Sonson went on to explain that his father lived and worked on Martinique, an island in the Caribbean, to provide for his family. He said, "My mom found out that he has another family in Martinique." His eyes fell to the ground. "When I was four years old, my dad came home to visit, but I cried and did not go to him because I did not recognize him." He shared that he had essentially lost his father and had grown up without a father figure.

The destruction and futility that sin inflicts on individuals, families, and societies was tangible that evening. However, Sonson went on to explain that he would never be victim to his circumstances. "My father is an example of the man that I will never be."

He continued, "You know, Kristine, it takes a lot of work and discipline to reach your dreams. But if you are willing to suffer, you will reach them." With determination and hope in his eyes, he added, "My dream is to become a doctor!"

I admired Sonson's hope and determination, but I wondered what kind of obstacles Sonson would need to overcome in a developing nation. And I wondered how much suffering Sonson would be willing to endure to reach his dream of becoming a doctor.

At the gate that evening, as the sun was setting, I called out, *"Pase bon nwi timoun'm yo."* (Have a good night, my children.) Before they left, the kids asked for a goodnight kiss. I placed a kiss on each of their beautiful foreheads.

One scorching day, we loaded up as usual into the Kawasaki "mule"—a quad with two rows of seats and a cargo bed in the back. We drove to a church and set up our clinic. After treating fifty patients with bacterial, viral, and fungal ailments, the doctor, translators, pharmacist, and I loaded up our large plastic containers of medications and supplies. We crammed in and drove down the dirt road. We merged onto the main highway in Léogâne. Huge semis roared by us as we treacherously drove on the edge of the highway with traffic. I had heard that many deadly motorcycle and car accidents occurred on this highway. *Would we be next?* I closed my eyes and desperately prayed.

"Why aren't we taking the backroads?" I shouted out above the cacophony.

"Because this way is faster," Wilfried answered.

Of course, I thought. *Getting there quickly is more important than arriving safely.*

Finally, we arrived at the compound. Wilfrid honked the horn a few times, and the security guard opened the heavy gate.

I jumped out of the mule and made my way to the bathroom for a cold shower. Cold water washed away the dirt and diesel fumes. Suddenly, endearing voices came from outside the gate: "Kristine! Kristine!"

I smiled. *My children.*

The children knew when the VBS started, but some always arrived early. I grabbed the children's Bible, looked through it, and prepared a lesson for my *timoun yo* (children). By now, many children had congregated at the gate for a time of Bible lessons, learning English, and playing games. I opened the front gate, and they shouted with joy. I joined them in their celebration, jumping and shouting with them.

"Okay, okay, children—sit down, please," I said. Sonson stood by and translated. "Today, we will learn some stories in the Bible." I looked around at my children and envisioned them becoming great leaders for their generation. Most of the children were boys, and I knew that these boys would soon become men and leaders in their home.

Under the mango tree, we learned about David's great faith in God and his deliverance from the hand of the Philistine. Their eyes widened when we explained that after David defeated the Philistine with a sling and a stone, he decapitated the giant's head with his own sword (1 Samuel 17:51).

We discussed that with God all things are possible. Together we exclaimed with our fists in the air, *"Avèk Jezi nou genyen pouvwa!"* (With Jesus we have power!) I loved seeing their excitement to learn God's Word and how it could be applied to their lives.

Before Wilfrid went home for the night, he stopped by our group.

"Why do you let them come over like that?" he asked and pointed to their dusty clothing with holes.

"Because they're poor," I replied. It seemed obvious to me.

"Just because they're poor doesn't mean they have to be dirty," he responded.

That thought had never occurred to me. So, after the Bible lesson I told the children that before they came over, they needed to take a bath. After our talk that evening, in the following days, they proudly revealed the white residue of baby powder on their chests.

Our month of serving in Haiti ended far too soon. On my last evening, the children gathered together and sang "This Is the Day" in Haitian Creole. Their melody traveled to my heart. I went home, but I left my heart in the beautiful and dusty streets of Léogâne.

Reflection

- In what ways have you seen God's guidance in your life?

- In what ways do you need God's guidance in your life? Write out a prayer asking for His direction.

Meditation

Trust in the Lord with all your heart, and do not lean on your own understanding. In all your ways acknowledge him, and he will make straight your paths (Proverbs 3:5-6).

The Lord is my shepherd; I shall not want (Psalm 23:1).

And the Lord will guide you continually and satisfy your desire in scorched places and make your bones strong; and you shall be like a watered garden, like a spring of water, whose waters do not fail (Isaiah 58:11).

Chapter Seven
Throwing Rocks

To the world you may be one person—
but to one person, you may be the world.
(Bill Wilson)

The precious baby in Minneapolis became stronger. She underwent cardiac surgery, and therefore no longer needed a tracheostomy or ventilator—which also meant she no longer needed nurses. My time in Minneapolis came to an end.

I asked Bayada if they would be willing to send me back to Haiti for four months, and they agreed. However, I knew that if I went to Haiti, I would need to forfeit the college courses I had already signed up for. *Would I also need to forfeit my dream of furthering my education and becoming a registered nurse?* I asked my dad what he thought, and as in years prior, he suggested that I seek Pastor Steve's counsel.

I sat in the youth pastor's office once again. He asked me about my mission trip to Haiti. I started to form a reply but suddenly, as if floodgates collapsed, tears began to pour down my face.

I was surprised at my emotional reaction and tried to explain through the tears. I told him about my children in Léogâne—how they came over every day after clinic to learn about our Creator. I explained their need for guidance and love.

"I could serve in Haiti for four months," I said, "or I could go back to college this spring and be more equipped as a registered nurse."

I thought about a phone call I had received from my children a few weeks prior. They were sobbing over the phone and, through their tears, I heard, *"Nou sonje ou!"* (We miss you!) My heart ached. *If I wasn't there to protect and lead them, who would? Yet wouldn't it make sense to be more equipped and to receive more training?* My racing thoughts were interrupted.

"Kristine," he said. "Those kids need you."

I was shocked. I was expecting him to give me the seemingly logical advice to return to college. Instead—as if God's words were flowing from his mouth—he said, "You need to go back to Haiti."

My eyes were glazed over, but my situation could not be more clear. I thanked him and left his office.

On the drive home, hope and clarity became my resolve. My children were like sheep, and I would tend to them. I was reminded of Jesus' heart for those around Him: "When he saw the crowds, he had compassion for them, because they were harassed and helpless, like sheep without a shepherd" (Matthew 9:36).

I returned to Haiti and to the same Heart to Heart compound in Léogâne. After serving in the mobile clinics, my children lined up outside the gate waiting for me to let them in. During our time together, volunteer doctors and nurses sat with us under the mango tree and watched the *blan* girl teach the children Bible lessons, hygienic practices, and English.

I continued to pray every day, asking God to give me the ability to speak and understand their language. There were ten million people in Haiti, and I desperately wanted to share Jesus with the Haitians in their language. By God's grace, day by day the words flowing from the children's mouths began to make sense, and I began to relay biblical truths to them directly.

My vision was to raise up leaders. At the beginning of class, I assigned one of the children to be a *pwofesè* (teacher) for the day. My children waved their hands in the air, hoping to be called on. After I chose a teacher, I pulled him or her off to the side, and went over the lesson plan for the day. And then I stood off to the side as he or she led the lesson.

As the Bible lessons carried on, Joseph sat on the bench, stone cold. His arms were over his chest as he faced the compound wall. *Attitude* was written all over his face.

I asked the group what they wanted to be when they grew up. They stood up one at a time and answered: doctor, nurse, teacher, engineer.

I asked, *"Joseph, kisa ou vle fe?"* (Joseph, what do you want to be?)

"Alonanai," he responded, and the kids broke out giggling.

I asked Sonson, "What does *alonanai* mean?"

"He wants to be a gangster," Sonson said. Joseph's face cracked into a grin. He seemed pleased with his response and his peers' reaction.

I looked back at Joseph and saw the painful wounds of a broken home. *If he had a mother and a father lovingly guiding him, would he still want to be a gangster?*

"Joseph, ou konnen ou te kòmanse sa." (Joseph, you know that you started this.) He met my eyes briefly, but he quickly turned toward the wall. I was determined to break through. *"Chak jou tout timoun yo vini paske ou menm!"* (Every day the children come because of you!) His gaze remained transfixed on the wall.

I had a mission: I would break through to Joseph, and I would do so with love and concern. Above all else, he would know that he is loved.

One day after clinic, I announced, *"Jodia, Joseph se pwofesè!"* (Today, Joseph will be the teacher!) I had already planned to make gospel bracelets, and I asked Joseph to explain what each color bead represented. I stood back and witnessed my proclaimed want-to-be gangster teach the children that black represented sin, red was for Jesus' blood, white meant purity, and green signified growing in Christ. The children tied the beaded bracelets around their wrists, and Joseph's face lit up with a smile. He seemed proud that he had done something good.

Joseph wasn't the only child without a mom. Annel was another precious boy who suffered this reality. Sonson explained to me that his mother had died in the earthquake and that his dad cared for him.

One afternoon, I saw Annel's father outside the compound. The sun's UV rays had left its damage on the deep creases of his weathered skin. He was lean, yet muscle jutted out as he gripped a rope. The rope was tied around a large heifer, whose every rib protruded from underneath its hide. Annel's father tugged relentlessly to keep it coming after him. He looked up briefly, smiled, and waved.

"Bonswa," I said. I wondered if he loved Annel. I wondered if he was able to provide for Annel's basic needs. Annel was thin and

didn't appear to be getting the daily nutrition he needed. When he spoke, it was more like mumbling than coherent words.

One morning, as we drove the Kawasaki mule to clinic, we saw Annel sitting in the dirt and weeping on the side of the road. I looked around—many people were near him, but no one attended to his pain or sorrow. He was completely ignored.

"Please stop the car," I said. I pushed past the apathetic observers. I wanted to scold them, but instead knelt next to Annel in the dirt and held him in my arms. It was all I could do to not weep with him. I didn't know what had caused his tears, but it was becoming clear that Annel was hungry and neglected. I pressed some dollar bills in his hand. Later, I gave Annel clothing, money for school, and a soccer ball.

I knew he needed more than that, and that these were only small actions, but I wanted Annel to know that he was loved and cared for not only by me, but more importantly by Jesus.

One afternoon, after clinic, I welcomed the children as usual through the gates, and one of the girls asked the most bizarre question.

"Èske ou se Jezi?" (Are you Jesus?)

I was taken back. *"Non, mwen pa se Jezi!"* (No, I'm not Jesus!)

She explained to me that people in the community were saying that Jesus had come to their community, and that I was Him. I thought of the many reasons that I couldn't possibly be Jesus. *However,* I thought, *is this what it means to portray Jesus' love to people around us? Does it mean to love people so deeply, so genuinely, that they would actually see Jesus through us?* I was putting a drop in a vast ocean, an ocean that had many needs and great suffering. *One child at a time,* I told myself.

As precious as I knew my children were, I also saw fire in their souls. They seemed more passionate, more fierce than the children back home. I figured that this spirit of determination must have permeated the Haitians who overthrew their French occupiers in 1803. These Haitians fought for their independence, and after the death of almost half the population and the burning of their country (including all the trees), the Haitians stood tall, becoming the first successful slave revolt in history.[8] It seemed that this spirit of determination had been passed on through the centuries, or maybe it had been wrought from the constant oppression of their corrupt government and daily afflictions. Whatever the reason, Haitians seem to carry this same fire, including my precious children.

One week, I was assigned to serve in the mountainous countryside of Cascade Pétion. I informed my children that I would return the following week, but after my time of cultural immersion in the mountains, Dr. Spaulding informed me that the children had made demands on the other volunteers who were stationed in Léogâne. The children wanted access to the compound but were denied. They had then decided to pick up rocks and throw them over the fence. I was appalled and feared that Heart to Heart wouldn't allow them back in.

When I returned to Léogâne, I confronted them about their behavior. I reminded them of what a privilege it was that Heart to Heart allowed us to come together. I decided to create more ground rules. If any of the children broke the rules, then they would need to leave the compound. Some of the rules included no throwing of rocks and no eating of hair. The children laughed at the last rule. However, I had seen the kids grabbing at their companions' tight curly hair with their teeth, then yanking back to tear the child's hair. Even at a young age, it was clear that everyone's nature is bent toward sin. For the most part, they followed these new rules.

As I continued to teach the children, I wondered if they were old enough to learn about the important concept of purity. One evening, as they sat on the chairs and looked up at me, I asked them if they were ready to learn about purity. Without hesitation, they told me they wanted to learn more and were already aware of that concept. *Who was teaching them? The media? Their friends? Or perhaps, hopefully, their family and their church.*

I began discussing the importance of keeping themselves pure for their future spouse. I explained that keeping themselves for their future spouse requires patience and strength that can come only from Jesus.

I told them, *"Jezi ap ede non chak jou."* (Jesus will help us every day.)

I pointed to my sterling silver ring on my left index finger and explained that it represented a commitment I made to wait for my future husband.

My children explained to me that they didn't know anyone else who waited for their spouse—only me. My heart sank. They needed godly examples to show them that living for the Lord in a sinful world is possible. I was glad, by God's grace, to show them that it is possible.

One day the children came over with an interesting proposal. They said, *"Jodia nou pral beyen. Èske ou vle vini tou?"* (Today we're going to take a bath. Would you like to come too?) Anticipation oozed from their eyes.

I replied, *"Wi! Mwen vle vini tou."* (Yes! I would like to come too.) I wondered what this bathing adventure would entail.

After driving for several minutes, Sonson parked the truck on the side of a paved road. I looked around and noticed a concrete trench next to the road. Powerful spouts of water shot from the side of a large building. *Where was this water coming from? Did they know the source, or even care?*

My children jumped off the truck bed, and without hesitation jumped into the trenches with huge smiles on their faces. A car tire sat in their bathing area. They grabbed a bar of soap and began lathering their bodies. Their dark brown bodies were covered with white suds. I shared in their joy. However, it wasn't quite normal to me and even a little sad.

After four wonderful and laborious months, my time in Haiti came to an end. Although I would always miss my children, I knew that my purpose and mission was complete. Before I left, I encouraged them to continue growing in their love for the Lord by attending church and reading His Word.

My children's eyes glazed over with tears as we said our goodbyes. I tried my best to implement the strength they had shown me. Once again, I left Haiti, but my heart would stay with them.

After I boarded the plane and we took flight, I looked out my window at the immaculate clouds and ocean. I grabbed my journal and wrote: *What a privilege it was to tend to God's flock in Haiti. What a privilege it was to be on mission for my Lord.* There was nothing I wanted more than to be a vessel of God's truth and love.

Suddenly I felt a tug on my heart about something else—or rather, *someone*. My children had asked me why I was single. I told them, *"Paske, Maryèm bezwen renmen Ayiti."* (Because my husband needs to love Haiti.) With this answer, they simultaneously shouted out for joy.

After this mission, I so badly wanted to rest my head on a man's shoulder—my husband's shoulder—but he wasn't there. I continued writing: *Lord, I feel as if he is thousands of miles and an ocean away.* I opened my Bible and read Joshua 1:9: "Have I not commanded you? Be strong and courageous. Do not be frightened, and do not be dismayed, for the LORD your God is with you wherever you go."

Wait patiently for him, I told myself.

Reflection

- In what ways have you seen God's strength in your life? In what areas do you need His strength?

- What would you say is the current mission that God has you on?

____

____

____

____

____

____

____

____

____

Meditation

> Be on your guard; stand firm in the faith; be men of courage; be strong (1 Corinthians 16:13).
>
> David also said to Solomon his son, "Be strong and courageous, and do the work. Do not be afraid or discouraged, for the LORD God, my God, is with you. He will not fail you or forsake you until all the work for the service of the temple of the LORD is finished" (1 Chronicles 28:20 NIV).
>
> The LORD is my light and my salvation; whom shall I fear? The LORD is the strength of my life; of whom shall I be afraid? (Psalm 27:1 KJV).

Our team to Ghana, June 2007

A meal for a village in northern Ghana

Another village we went to for a feeding

A fifth grade class in Accra, Ghana

Fun in the class

A well for a village in northern Ghana

Hannah, my adventure friend

Heidi caring for Canid, the baby in Mozambique

A mother's hope for her little girl

Fred

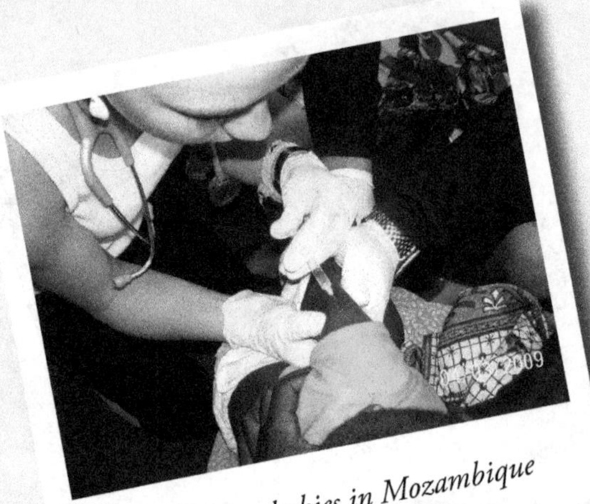

Immunizing babies in Mozambique

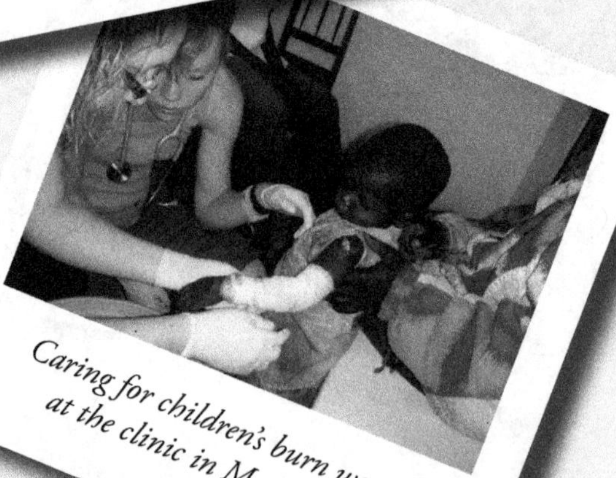

Caring for children's burn wounds at the clinic in Mozambique

Suzanne

My children in Léogâne

Bible study

Joseph

Annel

Teaching the kids under a mango tree

The strength of Haiti

The beauty of Haiti

My children

Taking a bath on the side of a road

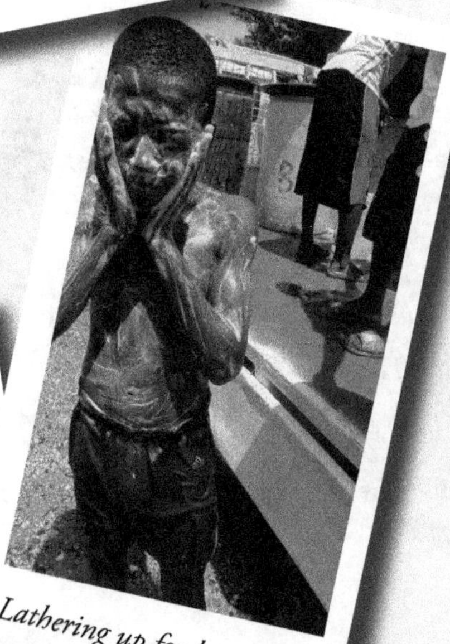

Lathering up for bath time

Sonson is studying medicine in the Dominican Republic. Soon he will reach his dream and become a doctor.

Dr. Spaulding

The kids are shouting out in Haitian Creole, "With Jesus we have power!"

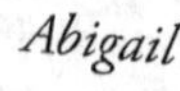

Abigail

Chapter Eight
Difficult Surrender

But this command I gave them: 'Obey my voice, and I will be your God, and you shall be my people. And walk in all the way that I command you, that it may be well with you.'
(Jeremiah 7:23)

"What was that?" I called out to my Alaskan friend paddling just ahead of me. As we were kayaking on the peaceful waters of Lake Marquette in central Minnesota, Michelle had made a loud, high-pitched sound—a noise I'd never heard before.

"It's an eagle call," she replied, looking up to the sky. "It's the sound of a dying rabbit."

I grinned. I was learning that my new Alaskan friend had some unique and impressive skills.

After returning home from my four-month mission to Haiti, I applied and was accepted into Bemidji State University, located three hours from my parents' home. I planned to continue my nursing education and reach my dream to become a registered nurse.

I was about to begin searching for apartments in the area when my dad mentioned that Oak Hills Christian College was also located in Bemidji. "You should contact them," he said, "and see if you can live there while you attend college."

"Dad, I don't think they'll let college students from a secular college live in their dorms," I replied.

My dad seemed determined, and he contacted the president of Oak Hills College. To my surprise, I could live there. I contacted the president, and he explained that this would be the first year that Oak Hills Christian College would accept students from Bemidji State University and Northwest Tech, the two secular colleges in the area.

At the end of August, I moved into a girls' dorm at the Christian college. It seemed surreal that a Christian college would allow students from other colleges to live in their dorms, but I was thankful for their open arms and the chance to be surrounded by a body of believers. During my first week, the dorm director told me to make myself at home and attend chapel or any other event that the college hosted, so I did just that. The campus was a beautiful and peaceful environment situated on a large tree-covered acreage, and the dorms overlooked Lake Marquette.

The college also offered kayaks for their students to use at leisure. When I heard about this, I asked Michelle, an Oak Hills student whom I had met in the cafeteria the first week of college, if she would like to join me. As we paddled across the still water, I prayed for my children in Haiti that I had left just three months prior. Our paddle out that day marked the beginning of our friendship, and throughout the semester we became good friends.

As I lived in the dorm and watched classmates around me

falling in love and getting engaged, I desired to be in a relationship too, but I understood to some extent, that being with the wrong man would be worse than the struggles of singleness. But that truth didn't ease the aching pain of loneliness that occasionally reared up or the sharp temptation to compromise.

One day in the library after class, one of my classmates approached me. "That Christianity thing just isn't for me," he grinned. He looked into my eyes, waiting for my reaction.

We sat down at a table, and he went on to explain his stance as an atheist. After his explanation of science and the views of highly regarded atheists in the secular community, I shared my beliefs. As we conversed, I was drawn deeper into his charismatic personality. We started hanging out, and like a slippery slope, we became physically affectionate. *It's just kissing,* I told myself. *I'm still keeping myself for my husband.* I tried to reassure my tormented conscience.

I told a Christian friend about my struggle, and she told me that giving myself away could happen in a matter of seconds. "Be careful," she said. "You're playing with fire and trying to not get burned."

I was beginning to realize that God created sex to be an activity that *quickly* progresses. To build a fire of passion and then try to stop would be like trying to put out a wildfire. And building this fire with a man who wasn't my husband couldn't possibly be part of God's original design.

I asked Michelle to keep me accountable, but accountability without a willingness to change is pointless. I knew that God's Word said that there shouldn't be a hint of sexual immorality in the midst of God's people, but I felt trapped in my desire. I was walking on a path that was leading me further from my commitment.

I went to a Monday morning chapel at the Christian college. The worship team began singing "Long Black Train" by Josh Turner. Suddenly, everything seemed to disappear around me, and the words of the song traveled to my soul and brought truth into my darkness. The bass tone of the worship leader's voice thundered through the speaker:

> "There's an engineer on that long black train
> making you wonder if your ride is worth the pain.
> He's just a-waitin' on your heart to say,
> Let me ride on that long black train."[9]

Like a lightning bolt, I understood that I was on a train with Satan as the conductor. I knew he wanted nothing more than to see me fall so he could bring condemnation and ultimately taint my Creator's glory. I began to desperately pray while the worship leader sang. *O Jesus, take me off this train! I can't get off myself…*

I went back to my dorm room and listened to the song over and over again. I was desperate for strength, but I couldn't find it in myself. As the words reverberated through my laptop speakers, I began to feel a small yet powerful strength rise up in my being. Then I remembered a verse: "For God has not given us a spirit of fear, but of power and love and self-control" (2 Timothy 1:7). Things became clear. I would get off the train—but only with God's strength.

I contacted the friend and ended the ungodly relationship. I explained to him that I needed to cut all ties because any contact would cause temptation that I couldn't handle. Upon reflection, I realized that our interaction shouldn't have gone farther than simply sharing the gospel. Instead, I had compromised and justified my actions. But I learned that sin—no matter how pleasurable or desirous it seems—will always lead to consequences and death. I asked God for forgiveness and determined that my next kiss would be for my future husband. I was thankful for His constant faithfulness: "If we confess our sins, he is faithful and just to forgive us our sins and to cleanse us from all unrighteousness" (1 John 1:9).

I finished the intensive nursing studies at the college and passed the NCLEX-RN. With this new license, I returned home to enjoy the warm summer days in Minnesota with my family as I applied to hospitals in the area. My Minnesota home was a place where my heart knew I could always come back to. My parents welcomed me there, and I appreciated their love and support. But as my single days dragged on longer than I expected, I became restless about living in my parents' basement.

On a summer day, my niece and nephew came over to my parents' house. My nephew swung on our tree swing supported by a strong oak tree. As he swung, his hand went up to touch the sky and then came back down again. While Minnesota has some of the harshest winters, the summers and family are the reason so many people stay. Extra hours of sunlight fill the days, and fields and gardens produce vibrant crops and fresh vegetables. While many Minnesotans "hibernate" throughout the winter, the summer days teem with life as we drink in every ounce of warmth and sunshine.

I loved spending time with my parents and niece and nephew, and while everything seemed perfect on the outside, I felt a war in my soul. Tears welled up in my eyes, and I quickly withdrew to my room downstairs. My dad must have sensed that something was wrong and followed me.

A simple journey and decision made as a teenage girl abounding in hope and innocence suddenly felt like an impossible undertaking. As I met the threshold of my room, tears filled my eyes and streamed down my face. I began to sob. Tears glided down my face like sharp icicles as I felt the gnawing pain of my heart's desire unmet, my vision unseen, and my goal out of reach.

My dad asked me what was wrong. His eyes spoke of his genuine concern.

"Dad, I thought I would be married by now," I said through my sobs. "I'm living in yours and Mom's basement. I'm twenty-seven years old. I'm not even sure my future husband exists. Why am I waiting? I can't do this anymore!"

My dad looked troubled to see me in this state. "Does it just suddenly hit you?" he asked. He seemed to be genuinely trying to understand where these intense emotions were coming from.

"Yeah," I said. "I just can't do this anymore!"

"Hold on," he said. "He *will* be worth it." Lovingly and compassionately, my dad reassured me.

I didn't expect a sudden change in my intense feelings, but my dad's words brought immediate courage and resolve. I swallowed back my tears and believed my dad—that my future husband would be worth not just the wait, but also the struggle.

After our conversation, I sat down on my bedroom floor and began to write a love letter to my future husband. A tear fell down my face and stained the paper as I wrote:

> To my beloved, I've been thinking about you a lot lately. When will it be okay for us to be together? It gets so hard to wait for you. The Lord has told me that I am

> to wait patiently. So, I am. I am waiting patiently. I feel like I have been waiting forever. I just can't wait to say, "I love you" to you. It's hard to wait because I want to hold your hand. It's hard to wait because I want to wake up next to you in some crazy country or at least in the same bed. It's hard to wait for you because I want to know you deeply, and I want to be known deeply. I am waiting patiently with anticipation. Come quickly, or rather come in God's perfect timing. My eyes, heart, mind, and soul are all for you. I hope God's plan is to give you to me soon, but I would wait forever for you. I miss you, and I love you. Love, Kristine.

I placed the letter in a scrapbook with other letters I had written to a man I had never met.

I was thankful for my parents' constant support. Proverbs 11:14 tells us, "Where there is no counsel, the people fall, but in the multitude of counselors there is safety." My parents' support helped tremendously, but the struggle did not subside.

One night at home, the stinging pain of loneliness felt so great that I couldn't sleep. Thoughts of a lifetime of singleness flooded my mind. The wait to be united with my husband was becoming exponentially more difficult with each passing year.

Earlier that night, I had listened to a sermon online. The pastor explained that as a person gets into their late twenties, singleness becomes a form of suffering. He validated the feelings that I was experiencing.

In desperation, I grabbed my phone and searched the Internet for a Christian chat helpline. I explained my difficulty to the life coach. I'm sure that the person meant well, but the advice I received didn't help. They asked if I had a boyfriend, and I typed back *no*. The comment in response was something along the lines of "Then why are you worried?" I was stunned. *Does this person not know that sexual immorality is everywhere—easily accessible—and that society is constantly telling us to go for it?*

I got offline. I tossed and turned all that night. I should have gone to Jesus and received His strength and peace through His Word, but I was at the end of my rope and felt so weak.

Suddenly, through the curtains of my bedroom window, brilliant orange rays of light began to stream through—the sign of a new day. I got up and moved the curtains aside to see the brilliance of a sunrise. In that moment, verses flowed into my mind: "The steadfast love of the LORD never ceases; his mercies never come to an end; they are new every morning; great is your faithfulness" (Lamentations 3:22-23). The war that terrorized my soul calmed to a slow and steady resolve as I continued looking through my window at the beautiful sunrise.

Perhaps God is calling me to a life of singleness. If this is Your calling, then You will be enough. Lord, my life is Yours.

I felt strength rise up in the core of my being. I knew that the source of this strength was the result of His abounding mercies that are poured out on His children every morning.

Reflection

- Is there a hurdle in your life that seems impossible to overcome? Have you prayed about and sought out Biblical counsel?

- Write out a prayer asking for God's strength to overcome and thank Him for His faithfulness.

Meditation

No, in all these things we are more than conquerors through him who loved us (Romans 8:37).

He will cover you with his pinions, and under his wings you will find refuge; his faithfulness is a shield and buckler (Psalm 91:4).

Let us hold fast the confession of our hope without wavering, for he who promised is faithful (Hebrews 10:23).

Chapter Nine

An Irrevocable Calling

When the will of God crosses the will of man,
somebody has to die.
(Addison Leitch)

"The pain starts here," he said and pointed to his right shoulder. "It goes across my chest. I'd rate the pain at level seven out of ten," the man said, as he sat on the ER gurney.

To clarify, I asked, "And this pain started last week? You went to the hospital, and you were told that it's a pulled muscle?"

"Yes, that's correct. But the pain hasn't gone away," he said.

"I'll be right back," I said. I rushed to Dr. Anokwute, who was fervently dictating on a computer. "Chest pain?" Dr. Anokwute said, meeting my eyes for a moment. "Do a full cardiac workup."

I hurried back to the ER room and completed an EKG. I started an IV in his right hand, filled test tubes with blood, and sent them off to the lab. Within minutes the results came back, revealing elevated cardiac enzymes.

"We need to fly him out," Dr. Anokwute instructed. I called the flight team, and they rushed through the ER doors within a few minutes. He was flown to a facility with a catheterization lab where he would receive the care he needed.

I made my way back to the ER nurses' station to document, and I looked over the electronic board that listed our current patients—each assigned a number based on their acuity. I sat down for a few moments to chart my assessment findings.

After obtaining my RN license and applying to hospitals in the area, LifeCare Medical Center contacted me for an interview, and I was hired. It was a privilege to provide care to people in the community and to work alongside amazing healthcare providers. But on the occasional slow day and on days off, I found my mind drifting off into the dusty streets of Léogâne, imagining myself walking alongside my beautiful Haitian children.

A few weeks prior, I had made the decision to travel to Haiti to visit my children for a week, and to do so without the covering of an organization. It was at the end of my week in Haiti that I looked into the dark eyes of my captor—the unmistakable desperation that marked them was unforgettable. But even more remarkable is the beauty that transcends and pierces through the darkness. I longed to call *Ayiti* my home.

On my days off work, I contacted Christian organizations and offered them one year of missionary nursing service. I waited anxiously to hear back. Then, week after week, emails arrived denying my request or having to deny the organization's request because of their far-reaching terms.

I didn't understand why they wouldn't accept my offer to serve long-term with their organization. I reasoned with myself as if my rationales would change my situation: *I know the language and customs, and I'd gladly follow their mission statement.* Dwelling on the rejection letters would be futile. *What if this door is closing? Would I accept a path that didn't lead to Haiti?* It seemed unlikely.

Suddenly, a strange thought surfaced. My oldest brother and his family had moved to Hawai'i. *Maybe I should apply for a RN position on O'ahu.* I searched online for pediatric home health nursing positions on the island. After scanning through several positions, I found one that struck my interest. I applied to the position, and a few hours later, received a notification that the office responded:

> I have read your résumé, and you seem to have the experiences that we are looking for. I also see by your cover letter that you are looking to relocate here to be closer to your brother and his family. Looking forward to working with you to make your move as easy as possible.
> –Mark

I stared at the email in disbelief. *Would it be possible that God is closing doors to Haiti and opening one to Hawai'i?* I shook my head. *No, that can't be possible.* It was improbable, and it posed as a major rut in my plans.

I went on a run to help sort out my thoughts. As I ran on the desolate gravel road outside my parents' home, tears began to stream down my face. "Lord," I prayed. "I want to go to Haiti, not Hawai'i." The tears stung as I imagined my Haitian children. "Please Lord, I want to serve in a developing nation—not paradise."

I didn't understand, but the doors to Haiti remained closed. I surrendered my desires and accepted the alternative path, although it seemed more foreign than the one that led to Haiti.

A couple of weeks later, I walked into Caribou Coffee, where the aroma of fresh coffee grounds and brewed coffee flooded my senses. That day, Abigail was working. Abby and I had grown up together in Warroad, Minnesota, and we had been friends since we were small. I came to the coffee shop not just for my pomegranate iced tea latte, but with an exciting offer.

"Hi, Abby! How are you?" I said. "I plan on moving to O'ahu this summer. Do you want to move there too and be roommates?"

"That sounds interesting," Abby replied. Her eyes sparkled with curiosity. "I'll definitely let you know," she said.

Waiting to hear back from Abby, I called Mary Joe, my former roommate in Minneapolis, and told her about my plans. I asked her if she would be interested in moving to Hawai'i.

"You know," she said. "I've been looking for the next adventure, and moving to Hawai'i would be the perfect place," she responded. Her twenty-year-old spirit had not faded.

My brother and his family checked out an apartment for us in Wahiawa, central O'ahu. After filling out an application, the landlord called. After explaining to me that people often have two jobs just to survive costly island life, he accepted our application.

I said goodbye to my lovely coworkers at LifeCare Medical Center and purchased a one-way ticket to O'ahu.

As the vast Boeing 737 jet flew smoothly above the Pacific Ocean, I looked outside the jet's window to the luminous white clouds and endless ocean. Everything was still and at ease—except my heart.

What am I doing? Why am I flying to Hawai'i? It seemed strange to be traveling without a clear mission or purpose. At least in Haiti I knew *why* I went. There was, however, one thing that I was certain of—and that was my timeline. One year from now, at the end of the apartment's lease, I would be off the island.

I thought about everything I needed to do to get situated: move into the apartment, start a new job, find a car, find a church, and find Christian friends.

My dad and I had been searching for used vehicles online and had contacted several people to inquire more about their cars. I had also been searching for churches online but hadn't decided on a specific one to visit.

I felt anxious and nervous about everything I needed to get in order. I prayed silently, asking for God's provision, and I was thankful that my parents decided to come along to help.

After several hours, the airplane thudded to the tarmac. Thick air swept through the cabin as the flight attendants opened the door. At the luggage carousel, I gathered my two suitcases, the extent of my belongings. My parents and I picked up the rental car at the airport and drove to an apartment complex on top of a hill called Wahiawa Heights. I breathed in the cool air of the higher elevation.

Hibiscus bushes and palm trees lined the entrance of my new home. I unlocked the front door. Mirrors covered entire walls ceiling to floor, creating an illusion of more space in the two-bedroom apartment. I found my bedroom and set down my belongings in the middle of the floor.

All right! Home, check! Next would be a vehicle.

My parents and I continued our search of used car ads. I wanted a smaller SUV priced under $5,000. Not wanting to appear overly picky to my parents, I didn't tell them that what I really wanted was a white Honda CR-V. Years earlier, I had seen Mary Joe's CR-V in Minneapolis; it seemed like a dependable vehicle, and she always spoke highly of it.

We looked at a Ford Escape, a Toyota Rav4, and an SUV that belonged to a surfer who couldn't recall when the last oil change was done. It was obvious that his vehicle was a mode of transportation to get him to and from one destination—the beach.

After three days, our options were waning, and discouragement began to seep in. The rental car was due back in the afternoon, and there was still no promising vehicle in sight. I called the car rental place to extend the lease for one more day.

The next day, a couple of hours before the rental vehicle was due back, my dad received a call.

"Hello," my dad said. "I'm sorry, what vehicle is this? Oh, the Honda CR-V? Yes, we were in Minnesota when I called. We're on the island now."

I stood next to my dad, hardly able to contain my excitement. We drove to meet the vehicle's owner at the Pearlridge Center shopping mall. We found her and her white CR-V in the busy parking lot.

After introductions, we jumped into the car and took it for a cruise. We sailed smoothly down Interstate H-1 as she explained that she was the original owner and serviced it only at Honda.

"I actually don't want to part from this vehicle," she said. "However, I bought a newer CR-V for my mom, and she isn't able to take it. So, I have to sell this vehicle and take the newer Honda."

"Are you excited to have a newer Honda CR-V?" I asked, holding the steering wheel.

She shrugged her shoulders. "I really like this car. Oh, and the tires need to be replaced. I'm willing to take a few hundred dollars off."

When we got back to the parking lot, I counted out $3,400, and she handed me the title. I felt bad that she didn't want to part with her car, but I also knew that I would take care of her gem.

I was in awe that the Lord had provided a vehicle at the last minute and for far less than expected. Furthermore, it was the exact type and color that my heart desired.

I named the car Hope. Hope abounds in our Savior, and I was reminded that He cares for each of our needs and desires. As Romans 5:5 states, "And hope does not put us to shame, because God's love has been poured into our hearts through the Holy Spirit who has been given to us."

Reflection

- How have you seen God's provision in your life?

- Write down a prayer thanking God for past provision and present your requests to Him.

Meditation

For the gifts and the calling of God are irrevocable (Romans 11:29).

And my God will supply every need of yours according to his riches in glory in Christ Jesus (Philippians 4:19).

The lions may grow weak and hungry, but those who seek the LORD lack no good thing (Psalm 34:10 NIV).

Chapter Ten
An Unexpected Meeting

As the heavens are higher than the earth,
so are my ways higher than your ways
and my thoughts than your thoughts.
(Isaiah 55:9)

I sat on my new twin mattress nestled on the floor against the wall, and I stared at the white wall in front of me. Silence echoed off the walls and seemed to scream at me from all directions.

My parents had flown back to Minnesota. Knowing that Mary Joe and Abby would be joining me within a couple of months didn't help.

I needed to escape the silence, so I hopped into my car and ventured to the North Shore. I jumped into the blue waves and let the clear water roll over me. It was an adventure, and the beauty and water were incomparable, but my loneliness in paradise persisted.

I knew that what I really needed was to be involved in a church and to be surrounded by other believers. My brother had invited me to Calvary Chapel Pearl Harbor. I was thankful for his invitation, but I had declined because his church was far from where I lived. Plus, there were numerous churches in Wahiawa.

My second week on the island, I visited a local fundamental Baptist church down the road from my apartment. The people were warm and welcoming, but I didn't see any kids. And there were only two young adults in the small congregation. I desired to fellowship with peers I could relate with and to see the beauty and liveliness that children gush with.

A few days later, my brother Justin called.

"Kristine, you really need to check out Calvary Chapel Pearl Harbor," he said. "It's the church I went to when I was in the military. You'll really appreciate Pastor Derald's teaching."

Justin seemed to be on a mission to get me to attend his church. I was impressed with his unwavering persistence, and clearly, he wasn't going to give up.

"Yeah, I think I'll check it out," I responded, mainly to appease him. After saying goodbye, I googled the church. It was Thursday, and I found on their website that there was a Thursday evening young adults Bible study. *Maybe there are young people at the study who I could connect with.*

I typed in the church's address into my phone's GPS and drove for twenty minutes. "You have arrived at your destination," the GPS shouted. I swung into a parking stall and looked around the huge parking lot. The only building that stood out was Foodland. I double-checked the address. *This is the place, but where's the church?* I jumped out of my car to find it, but no church was in sight. I pressed a button on my phone to flash the time. 6:35 P.M. *Maybe I should just go home. I don't want to be the new person showing up late.*

Before heading back to my car, I went to an ice cream shop next to Foodland to see if anyone had heard of the church.

"Yeah! You just go past the shopping center," one man said. "It's at the far end of the parking lot."

I thanked him, rushed to my car, and drove to the other side. As I pulled around, a huge building came into view. A large dove logo hung above the logo for Calvary Chapel. *Yes!* I breathed out in relief, parked my car, and jumped out. I rushed toward the church doors.

Locked. I peered through the glass doors. It was dark and empty.

I jogged to the side of the building and saw double doors wide open with light streaming out. As I approached this back entrance, a tall, good-looking man was walking out. My GPS continued to deliver directions toward the grocery store; I fumbled it around and silenced it. I looked up and met the eyes of the man as he extended his hand to introduce himself.

"Hi, I'm David."

"Hi, I'm Kristine," I said.

Inquisitively, he asked, "Are you here for the young adults' Bible study?"

"Yes I am!" I said, relieved that he knew about the Bible study.

"It will be starting shortly," he said and directed me to go through the gym and up the stairs. I thanked him and walked over to the gym. People were playing volleyball inside. It looked like a fun place.

I found the stairway and walked up to a large room with windows overlooking the gym. I peered over the volleyball teams and felt anxious to meet everyone in the study. After a few minutes, the game ended, and people started congregating in the upper room. David came in as well and greeted the group as he sat down and pulled out a guitar with sheet music.

We began to sing a familiar song, and I noticed an unmistakable passion emanate from him. After a worship set and introductions, he gave us instructions. After a portion of Scripture was read aloud, we could then express insight and application. It became clear that he was the leader of the Bible study.

I sat back and soaked in the study time. I knew that this was exactly what my soul needed—fellowship and God's living Word.

After the study, I grabbed my Bible, ready to set out, and with a plan to return on Sunday. David approached me as I gathered my belongings.

"So, what brought you to the island?" David asked. His look of inquisitiveness persisted.

"It's kind of a long story," I replied, and I thought about my children. "I wanted to live and serve in Haiti, but those doors closed. I have a brother on the island. I moved here two weeks ago."

"Haiti? And you've only been here for two weeks?" His eyes widened. "Welcome to the island! I definitely wanna hear your testimony sometime soon, and I would like to add you on social media." He asked for my full name.

I went to my car and suddenly the ache of loneliness melted away. I looked back at the church. It was already evident that a love for God and His Word flowed freely there. Going to church on Sunday would be my next adventure, and I couldn't wait to hear from the pastor.

On Sunday, I could almost see fire in the pastor's eyes as he declared from the pulpit, "God designed marriage between one male and one female. Homosexuality perverts God's original design. And it's not just homosexuality. Heterosexual sin is just as bad. Sex outside marriage is a defilement of the marriage bed!"

I felt the intensity of his message, and uneasiness slowly crept over me. I shifted my eyes around the sanctuary. *Are people going to storm out?*

He went on to speak about how the morality of our country is degraded. To my surprise, no one got up to leave. In fact, as he preached, no one seemed to move.

The service ended, and I stood up excited to see a genuine concern for lost souls. He had clearly addressed that sin was the entity that separates us from God, and that it needs to be removed for us to know our Savior.

I walked outside the sanctuary with some of my new friends, and I saw David in the foyer. The group began to formulate a plan for lunch.

"Yeah, let's get some grinds at Fatboy's!" David exclaimed.

I figured "grinds" meant food and was thrilled to hang out with my new friends. We arrived at a local diner, and I asked one of the girls what she recommended.

"You've got to try *poke*!" she responded.

She explained that it was a raw tuna dish. I ordered the *poke* and received a bowl with cubes of raw pink fish with seasonings sprinkled on top. A hot bed of rice, peppered with dried seaweed, sat underneath the raw tuna. I took my first bite. The smooth texture and burst of fresh taste exploded in my mouth. *Yes, this is island life!*

I looked to the end of the long table. David and his parents sat at the other end. I conversed with my new friends I had met just a few days prior. Their love for Jesus continued to be a breath of fresh air.

During the coming weeks, I received casual, friendly texts from David. I figured that since he was born and raised on the island, he was driven to make sure that I felt welcome. He told me that it was his mission to teach this *haole* girl one Hawaiian word a day. I learned that *hele* meant "go," *da kine* can mean just about anything, and that *na ka oi* means "it's the best." David's kindness made me feel welcome to the island, and he also got me excited to learn more about the Hawaiian culture.

I checked out books from the library to learn about the history of Hawai'i. I learned that in 1778, Captain Cook's crew—the first explorers here from Europe—came to Hawai'i. Though instructed not to intermingle with the islanders, they did so, and this uniting brought infectious diseases including STIs. These diseases killed the majority of the people.[10] The population of 250,000 Hawaiians in 1758 had dwindled by 1850 to only 84,000.[11]

In 1807, Henry Opu-kaha-'ia, a young Hawaiian, traveled to the U.S., received an education, and became a Christian.[12] Henry had a vision to bring knowledge of Christ back to his people who were still worshiping false gods. Meanwhile, in 1819, the ruling chief at the time—Liholiho, the son of King Kamehameha—told his people to destroy images of the Hawaiian gods and end their *kapu* system (a system of religious and social laws rooted in polytheism that had been upheld for generations).[13]

Henry died before his vision to preach Christ to his people was realized. However, in 1820, Christian missionaries inspired by Henry arrived and not only brought knowledge of Christ but literacy. From 1820 to 1832, the literacy rate for the Hawaiian population went from zero percent to ninety-one percent.[14] And with the *kapu* way of life annihilated, many of the *ali'i* (ruling chiefs) put their faith in Christ, and Christianity spread throughout the islands.

I was beginning to see that Hawai'i's history was not only vast but extreme. I also borrowed a book to learn some Hawaiian. When I went to the bank to set up an account, I decided to practice the words I had learned.

"Aloha! Pehea 'oe?" I said and waited for a response from the young man behind the counter.

Another counter attendant overheard the greeting, and I was met with blank stares. I quickly learned that Pidgin was much more commonly spoken among people than Hawaiian.

When David and I saw each other, we would greet one another by saying, "Braddah!" and "Sistah!" We would go to Bible study, hang out at Bible study group outings, and see each other at church. Through our friendship, I learned that David not only led the young adults Bible study but also taught Sunday school, helped out with youth group on Fridays, was a camp counselor in the summer, and was part of a Christian reggae band.

His heart for ministry and commitment to serve the Lord was intriguing, but I quickly dismissed my curiosity and set my heart to enjoy every tropical moment, knowing that I would be island bound for only one year.

Mary Joe and Abby eventually flew in for the grand adventure of island life. We all kept busy with work, but when we were all home, we enjoyed one another's company. Abby remained a loyal friend, and I knew she would always be there to provide a listening ear or to join me in venturing around the island. Mary Joe kept her upbeat and fun personality. One day, without her realization, I watched Mary Joe make a cup of coffee. She hummed and happily spoke to herself as she perfected her cup of joe. I was amused that she could make something so simple look like so much fun!

After several weeks of exploring the island, getting more settled in, and becoming closer with my new friends through the Bible study group, I received a phone call from David.

"Hi, David," I said. My heart began to pound faster. It was 3:05 P.M., five minutes after his shift ended at the shipyard. *Why was I on his mind right after work?*

"Hi, Kristine!" David exclaimed. "How are you? Are you enjoying island life?"

"Yes!" I replied. I explained my adventures to the North Shore.

"You have to check out Waimea Bay," he exclaimed. "You can jump off a huge rock there!"

"You're not the first person to recommend that," I replied. "I'll definitely check it out!"

After we hung up, I ran to Abby to tell her about the exciting phone call. "David called me," I exclaimed. "He's so encouraging! His encouraging attitude is going to bless his future wife so much."

She looked at me like, *Uh-huh, sure.*

"No, Abby we're just friends," I replied. But her same facial expression met my response.

One weekend, the Bible study group planned a hike up Koko Head. As we stood at the base of the hill, I looked up the railway path with no shade, no horizontal paths—just a steep constant incline to an unseen summit. It seemed intense enough, and we were all surging with excitement to take on this challenge. I turned to Abby.

"Are you ready?" I asked my friend.

With a huge grin she answered, "I am if you are!"

We began the trek up the railway track that once served as the means to deliver military supplies to personnel seventy-five years earlier, during World War II. Combined with the heat and the steep incline, Abby was having a bit of difficulty, so I stayed back with her. We stopped on the edge of the trail to guzzle down some water.

David noticed us falling behind the group and stayed back with us. The three of us slowly made our way up the hill. *What a sweet guy to stay with us!* As we moved closer to the summit, David handed out a gospel tract to a stranger. *He just gave that man the message of salvation!* I caught myself staring and wondered if my admiration for him was obvious.

After the hike, we piled into our vehicles to Teddy's Bigger Burgers and replenished the calories we'd burned through. David sat next to me at the restaurant.

I kept my cool as I found myself drawn to David's heart. It was obvious that he genuinely cared for the things of God, and he seemed to be ministering to people constantly. I tried to keep my guard up and my mind focused, but his calls, kindness, and heart were all so wonderful.

A few nights after the hike, I lay in bed, and thoughts of David flooded my mind. *Does he like me? No, we're just friends. He's a nice person. He's just being nice.* I tossed and turned, then grabbed for my phone. I aimlessly scrolled through social media. Suddenly a notification flashed on my screen.

Hey, Kristine! It was a message from David.

Why are you up so late? Another message flashed.

I looked at the messages. *I'm up because of you,* I thought. But I answered vaguely instead. He pressed to know why I was really up in the middle of the night. I gave another ambiguous reply, and he pressed to know more.

I typed back, *I'm having a hard time guarding my heart*. I didn't know if that was the right thing to do, but I figured that it was best to be honest and that my transparency might be what he needed.

A few days later David called again.

"Hi, Kristine! How are you?" he asked joyfully.

We talked at ease, simply as friends, as we discussed our jobs and island life.

Then his tone became more serious. "Kristine, I was hoping that I was the one on your mind that night you were up. We've been friends for a short while, but in the near future, I would like to enter into a courtship with you."

My heart began to race as I hung on to each word.

He continued, "Then I want to be engaged to you. I don't want these seasons to last too long. Ultimately, the goal is to be married to you. I won't be content with the title of girlfriend or even fiancée for you. I want you to be my wife."

My breath was taken away, and tears filled my eyes. I had waited so long to hear these words from a man—the words of pursuit and intention. To hear them now from David, a man whom I respected so much, was surreal. And I knew it was a rare thing for a man to state his intentions so clearly. I caught my breath to form a reply.

"I want that too," I said. "Thank you for being so straightforward with me."

"We'll allow the Lord to guide us," David said. "In this way, we'll know when and how to move forward with each season."

Suddenly, things were becoming clear. The purpose for flying to an island in the middle of the Pacific had been unclear to me but was understood perfectly by the One who was lovingly leading.

Reflection

- In what ways are you living out God's purpose for your life?

- Write out a prayer asking God to direct you toward His calling on your life.

Meditation

I cry out to God Most High, to God who fulfills his purpose for me (Psalm 57:2).

I know that you can do all things, and that no purpose of yours can be thwarted (Job 42:2).

Your word is a lamp to my feet and a light to my path (Psalm 119:105).

Chapter Eleven
This Man

A woman's heart should be so lost in God
that a man has to seek Him to find her.
(Maya Angelou)

The turquoise-blue waves thrashed against the wall of rocks that led to a cliff where I sat. *Lord, You are strong,* I prayed, as I watched wave after wave pound into the rock interface. The refreshing ocean mist rose magically to where we sat. Abby was next to me, looking at the waves below. The sky was a canvas of iridescent hues of orange and blue as the sun descended closer to the sea. *Your faithfulness, O God, reaches to the sky.*

I loved God's way of displaying His incomparable characteristics through creation. Abby and I were on an adventure on the west side of the island. We had fun climbing up the cliff, watching the sunset, and admiring God's majesty, but I found my mind drifting off as the sun hung just above the horizon.

I thought about David. I felt a steady patience and anticipation, wondering when we would become an official couple. I took in a breath of the misty oceanic air. *Is this the man You have for me, Lord?* David had stated his intentions of courtship and marriage two months earlier. We were in the "friendship season," which David had said "wouldn't last too long."

The more we spent time together as friends, the more I became intrigued by this man. At church, seeing David interact with the youth was endearing; he was impacting them and pointing them to Jesus at an impressionable time in their lives. David also faithfully led the young adults every Thursday evening—even after working all day at the shipyard. His passion for the Lord and to lead others to Him was unmistakable.

As the sun dipped below the horizon, Abby and I hiked along the rocky shore to make our way back to Mary Joe's hotel room. Mary Joe had booked one week at a hotel and had invited us to join her. With joy we accepted her invitation and stayed one night.

It was incredible to experience warmth in winter months, and Abby and I knew it wasn't something to take for granted as we soaked in the last ounces of warmth radiated in the twilight. We made our way to the hotel, chatted for a bit, ate, and crashed for the night.

As I drifted off into sleep, thoughts of David continued to circulate through my mind.

A couple of weeks later, David messaged my phone.

Hi, Kristine! Do you want to go to a movie? he asked. *Moana is showing.*

Sure! I replied.

I ran into our room and told Abby the exciting news. I got ready, rushed out the door, and met David at the theater.

As the movie progressed, the storyline blurred together. My heart pounded in my ears, and my stomach fluttered with thousands of butterflies. Suddenly, in the middle of the movie, David leaned toward me. My commitment to save my next kiss for my future husband flashed into my mind, and then I thought about David's phone call, telling me his intentions of marriage. I knew David was a man of his word—I leaned into his kiss, and in a split second, my heart became light, and I felt as if we soared through the air.

He asked me to be his girl, and I said yes.

When the movie ended, David walked me to my car. "I have a New Year's resolution," he told me. "My goal this year is to win your heart."

I smiled. I had been accustomed to guarding my heart, but I figured that my heart would soon be his. We kissed again.

As magical and exciting as those moments were, we failed to consider the door we had opened that would encourage physical closeness and desire for each other sooner than we could handle.

As the winter days rolled into spring, David displayed his love in creative ways. I taped his sweet love letters to the wall next to my bed and savored the sweet fragrance of flowers that occasionally filled our apartment. I placed the flowers next to my bed so I could wake up to this visual reminder of his love. At church and at the Bible study, David and I sat together. I imagined him one day leading our household closer to Christ.

During this season of growing in our relationship, we took personality tests to try to understand one another more. We also discussed our love languages to understand how we felt most loved.

A friend in Minnesota was on a similar journey as ours; she was also being pursued by a man of God, and their goal was marriage as well. One day she told me about something called the Prepare/Enrich Assessment. Pastor Wayne, my pastor at my home church in Minnesota, had provided it for my friend and her fiancé as part of their premarital counseling curriculum. I emailed Pastor Wayne and asked if he would be willing to send the assessment to David and me. He agreed.

We were instructed to take the assessments separately. Upon completion, the assessments were sent to Pastor Wayne, and we agreed to review our results with him in June. David and I were eager to learn those results.

David came over, and we waited eagerly for Pastor Wayne's call.

"Hi Kristine! And it's so nice to meet you, David. I'm Pastor Wayne."

After introductions, He explained to us that reviewing the results is normally done over a period of several premarital counseling sessions, but he was willing to give us a brief overview of our results in one session.

"This session will be a broad overview to see what strengths you have as a couple and what things you could work on," he added.

"The assessment determined that you are a vitalized couple," he explained. "This result identifies you as having the highest relationship satisfaction and the lowest rate of divorce."

Pastor Wayne then asked us questions to understand and encourage growth in a variety of areas in our relationship.

After saying goodbye to Pastor Wayne, David turned to me wide-eyed, "We're going to be a power couple! We'll be stronger together." He spoke with unshakable assurance.

I looked into my man's eyes and agreed. Christ's faithfulness resonated into the deep corners of my heart. For years I had prayed for David—but at that time David was only an idea, a concept, or at best a hope. Now before me was a man with a soul—a soul with a fire to know Christ and to make me his wife. As Proverbs 3:12 says, "Hope deferred makes the heart sick, but a desire fulfilled is a tree of life."

With this confirmation, the fire in my heart to know and to be known by my future husband was kindled even more. The door for physical closeness had been cracked open, and I longed to be closer yet. *But he's not my husband,* I reasoned with myself. I knew that his body belonged to one woman alone—his wife—just as my husband would have exclusive access to me. I didn't want to be a counterfeit version of his wife and take anything that did not yet belong to me. Also, I understood that desiring him before marriage would be lust rooted in selfishness, while desiring him in marriage would be love.

One evening he shared in tears about a past filled with selfishness and immorality. My heart broke over his pain and for our loss, but I knew that we could heal and move forward (2 Corinthians 5:16-17). However, red flags went up when he looked at or treated females in a way that made me uncomfortable. For the first time, I struggled with insecurity; but I tried to push those feelings aside because I trusted the man who held my heart. I also prayed and fasted for direction.

We desired to experience God's gift of intimacy in the correct context of marriage, and we understood that anything outside this context would have devastating effects on our relationship with God, with each other, and with those around us. We had many conversations about the importance of our purity, but we struggled to live out God's best. When we kissed each other passionately, afterward we felt the sharp conviction of not living with absolute purity.

Desperate for help, we sought accountability from friends and our mentor. Michelle, my Alaskan friend, sent me intentional texts asking me how we were doing with our boundaries. Leighton, our mentor, checked on us regularly and suggested that we not spend any time alone together. Another friend counseled us to do whatever it took to maintain our purity because we wouldn't want to live with that regret in our marriage.

We knew that the sooner we could get married, the sooner we could enjoy the gift of intimacy (1 Corinthians 7:2). But for now, we knew that the only way we would survive was to die to ourselves—to crucify our flesh. As Elisabeth Elliot said, "We are not meant to die merely in order to be dead. God could not want that for the creatures to whom He has given the breath of life. We die in order to live." [15] As Paul says in Galatians 2:20,

> I have been crucified with Christ and I no longer live, but Christ lives in me. The life I now live in the body, I live by faith in the Son of God, who loved me and gave himself for me.

It was becoming clear that purity would be possible only with God's strength, with our eyes locked on Christ. It meant not managing the flesh but crucifying it. And since Satan hates purity and desires all to fall and experience death, we would have to wield the weapons and put on the armor God had already given us.

Elisabeth Elliot also said the following that resonated with me:

> If there is an enemy of souls (and I have not the slightest doubt that there is), one thing he cannot abide is the desire for purity. Hence a man or woman's passions become his battleground. The Lover of souls does not prevent this. I was perplexed because it seemed to me He should prevent it, but He doesn't. He wants us to learn to use our weapons.[16]

Having faith in Him, believing in His Word, accepting truth over the enemy's lies, and putting on His righteousness—all this would be our battle gear. As Ephesians 6:11 says, "Put on the full armor of God."

Reflection

- Is there an area in your life that you find difficult to surrender to God?

- Write out a prayer to God asking for the strength to surrender and for wisdom in this area of your life.

___

___

___

___

___

___

___

___

___

___

Meditation

> Flee sexual immorality. Every other sin a person commits is outside the body, but the sexually immoral person sins against his own body (1 Corinthians 6:18).
>
> But sexual immorality and all impurity or covetousness must not even be named among you, as is proper among saints (Ephesians 5:3).
>
> Can a man scoop fire into his lap without his clothes being burned? Can a man walk on hot coals without his feet being scorched? So is he who sleeps with another man's wife; no one who touches her will go unpunished (Proverbs 6:27-29 NIV).

Chapter Twelve

An Important Question

A whole lot of what we call "struggling"
is simply delayed obedience.
(Elisabeth Elliot)

David pulled into the driveway, and I hopped in his passenger seat. We were going to a Saturday evening church in Honolulu called One Love, which had become a routine for us. It was the end of July, and we had been courting for about six months. Falling deeper in love with my man and with the Lord was more than exhilarating.

I looked into David's eyes as I buckled my seatbelt. It looked as if he was going to explode with excitement. I grinned. *Why is he so excited?*

David reversed the car out of the parking stall. The car bounced over the speed bumps. Suddenly, as if he couldn't contain his excitement any longer, David exclaimed, "Today I'm going to ask you the big question!"

I had to catch my breath. Then amusement overcame me. *Wasn't this supposed to be a surprise?*

"I hope it's okay that I told you!" he said with a huge grin.

"Oh, yes!" I said. "I'm glad to know. Then I can be prepared!"

Butterflies welled up in my stomach, and my mind began to race. *Me, engaged?* I looked down at my purity ring and twisted it around. The simple silver ring had left a small indent in my finger. *Has the day arrived where the one I love would ask me one of the most important questions?* Joy began to surge through my veins.

"I have to call your dad!" David said suddenly. "To receive his blessing."

He had asked for my dad's phone number months ago to state his intentions with me before we started our courtship. Now he scrolled through his contacts, found my dad's number, and called.

David turned on his speakerphone, and my dad answered, "Hi, David."

"Hi, Doug, how are you and Sonia? I'm calling you today to ask for your blessing. I would like to ask your daughter to marry me." David was still beaming.

We waited for my dad's response. In high school he had given me his blessing to serve on a foreign mission field and now I waited for him to give his blessing to the man whom I loved with all my heart.

My dad replied, "I know that you love the Lord and that you love my daughter dearly." He continued, "Do you promise to be faithful to my daughter and to always protect her?"

"Yes, I promise to be faithful to Kristine and to always care for her," David responded.

"Okay," my dad replied. "Yes, David—you have my blessing."

David and I looked at each other with huge grins. If my dad

only knew that I was listening. I wanted to yell out with excitement, *Dad, by the end of the evening, I'm going to be engaged!* But I held back.

My dad continued, "I know that my daughter will be in good hands."

David made a few more calls as we continued our drive to the church and spoke vaguely to the people on the other line. I tried to pick up on clues but couldn't piece everything together.

We pulled into the church parking lot and David turned toward me. "Do you want to see something?"

"Sure!" I said.

"Look in the middle console!" he exclaimed.

I opened the middle console and saw a delicate purple box.

"My ring is in there?" I asked, surprised.

"Yes! Do you want to see it? Actually no! You need to wait to see it!" he remarked.

I laughed again. We got out of our parked car, made our way to One Love, and sat toward the back—next to some of our dear friends.

Once the message concluded and the final song in worship was about to end, my heart started to race. *Is David going to ask right as church ends?* I looked to the row behind us and smiled at our friends. They didn't know that I knew the grand plan that they were involved in, but their grins could have given it away. The worship song ended, and David didn't get down on one knee. Instead he led me back to the parking lot.

We arrived back at David's car, and he went to his trunk, searching for something.

"Aha! Found it!" he exclaimed and came from the back of his vehicle with a sleeping mask.

"You need to wear this," he said, as he lifted the blindfold to my face while I sat in the passenger seat.

"Okay," I responded with a mixture of excitement and anticipation.

It was evening. The sun had already set, so everything felt extra-dark as I sat next to David. Double-checking that the blindfold was secure, David started his car and began to drive.

"Where are we going?" I asked, unable to contain my curiosity and excitement. "We're headed toward North Nimitz Beach!" I said, trying to gain a sense of direction.

"Not quite," he said in a mischievous tone.

Twenty minutes later, I felt the car veer right and could tell that we were on an off ramp. A few minutes later, we made a few turns and went over some speed bumps. Then the car came to a stop.

"We're here!" David said.

The speed bumps clued me in that we could be at Calvary Chapel Pearl Harbor, but I couldn't be sure. David's door shut and moments later, mine opened. His hand grasped mine, and he led me out of the car.

I stood next to his car with the sleeping mask still in place. "Let's take this off," he said.

My eyes adjusted, and a few feet in front of us, our friends lined up against a gate in front of Calvary Chapel. One of our friends held a guitar and started singing "Simplicity" by Rend Collective Experiment. I looked down to see rose petals and tea lights lighting our path.

Suddenly it felt like we were floating. David led me to the place where we'd met ten months earlier. As we walked, he told me about our first moments together.

"Almost one year ago, you were looking for a Bible study,"

David stated. "And you came to this church. As you approached the church, we met for the first time."

Then he knelt down, and my heart filled with sheer bliss.

"Kristine," he said, opening the purple box. The brilliant diamond ring couldn't outshine our hearts. "Will you marry me?"

"Yes!" I exclaimed.

He placed the most beautiful ring I'd ever seen on my left ring finger. The simple purity ring was replaced by a ring with precious gems.

After capturing the special moments with a Polaroid camera, we walked to a local restaurant next to the church. We were surrounded by our dear friends, and David placed a *haku lei* on my head that made me feel like royalty.

I felt like a Hawaiian princess. However, I didn't have my prince yet. With this new ring on my finger and deeper commitment established, my desire to be with him grew even more intense; the temptation had amped up. I prayed for strength and read God's Word. While in Proverbs, I read 10:29 (NKJV): "The way of the LORD is strength for the upright: but destruction will come to the workers of iniquity." According to this verse, walking in the Lord's statutes gave strength. I reasoned then that all strength belongs to those who follow Christ.

David and I had talked about getting a marriage license at the courthouse so we could ensure our sexual integrity. But when we considered our desire for our parents to witness our marriage ceremony, we decided to press forward and try to be patient. We discussed our situation with one another one afternoon, and our solution was to have a short engagement—a *very* short engagement. David proposed at the end of July, and we decided to plan for a September wedding.

Within a few days of our engagement, we went to our church to discuss our plans with the administrative pastor. We told him that we wanted a short engagement, and we also expressed our desire to schedule our big day in the church calendar. The administrative pastor advised us that it would be extremely difficult to pull off a wedding in a few short weeks.

"Okay," David and I said in agreement. Then David asked, "How about the first weekend in October?"

The administrative pastor agreed, and he marked down our day in the church schedule.

Now that our wedding date was set, we set our plans into overdrive. Planning a wedding in two short months would be nothing short of a miracle. Yet in the midst of our planning, we received blessing upon blessing as friends and family offered their services and talents to us.

Wendy, a family friend and an angel, came to our rescue when she offered to coordinate our big day. David and I met with her at Starbucks many evenings after work. We worked with Wendy on everything, from flowers, to the cake, to our theme. With the planning, Wendy also provided biblical insight on living out a godly marriage.

"You know," she said one evening, "I think it would be wise to take the first year of being married to build the foundation of your marriage. If you took one year off from ministry to build this foundation, I think you two would become an incredibly strong couple for the Lord in ministry." We appreciated her biblical insight and her strong administrative skills.

David and I felt the strain to pull off all the planning in eight weeks, but because of the body of Christ, our special day was coming together, detail by detail. Our vision was to have a simple and elegant wedding. We also desired to celebrate purity and the eternal union found in Christ. Essentially David and I wanted the Lord to be at the center of our entire celebration. To do this, we agreed that worship would be a major aspect of the ceremony. A beautiful couple offered to lead worship. They were so good that during our wedding rehearsal, Tyler, my middle brother, leaned over to my dad and asked, "Who hired the professionals?"

Not only did we survive the whirlwind of wedding planning, but God's strength enabled us to keep ourselves separate until our wedding night. We survived; however, our struggle was ultimately a matter of disobedience (1 John 2:16). When we surrender to God's Word and His Spirit, He empowers us to live holy lives as His pure bride: "For it is God who works in you both to will and to do for His good pleasure" (Philippians 2:13). And as Zechariah 4:6 tells us, "Not by might, nor by power, but by my Spirit, says the LORD of hosts."

A few days before my wedding, I packed my getaway bag. I looked forward to our big day and for our honeymoon. Soon I would be able to say, "Let him lead me to the banquet hall, and let his banner over me be love" (Song of Solomon 2:4 NIV).

Reflection

- What are some desires of your heart?

- Write out a prayer asking God to be the center of it all.

Meditation

> You shall love the Lord your God with all your heart and with all your soul and with all your might (Deuteronomy 6:5).
>
> But seek first the kingdom of God and his righteousness and all of these things will be added to you (Matthew 6:33).
>
> The kingdom of heaven is like a treasure hidden in a field, which a man found and covered up. Then in his joy he goes and sells all he has and buys that field (Matthew 13:44).

Chapter Thirteen
A Sacred Covenant

Let us rejoice and exult and give him the glory,
for the marriage of the Lamb has come,
and his Bride has made herself ready.
(Revelation 19:7)

"Lord, we thank You for bringing us together," David prayed with strength and sincerity. All I could see was the hem of his navy-blue suit arm. We held hands as he stood on the other side of the door. "May You receive all of the glory today and always in our lives. May our marriage be a constant light pointing others to You. In Your name we pray. Amen."

I loved hearing his voice, and the anticipation was heightened by my not seeing him. I longed to see my groom and present myself to him. After we prayed together, David went to the church's front stage, and I waited for my cue.

A few minutes later, the wedding coordinator's daughter waved me over. I walked over to the main doors of the sanctuary. Then the doors majestically flew open, and I saw him—the man with whom I was about to enter into the most sacred covenant. I held on to the arm of my dad, who had been the strongest support in my life. I floated down the aisle in a blissful state as the words of the song "Simplicity" played over the speakers:

> I come in simplicity longing for purity
> to worship You in Spirit and truth, only You.
> Lord strip it all away 'til only You remain
> I'm coming back, to my first love, only You.[17]

I looked out over the crowd. Our dear friends and family cheered us on with their smiles. Large Mason jars lined the aisle with white carnations and delicate baby's breath. The sanctuary had just the right amount of simplicity and elegance, and even the lighting made the sanctuary seem mystical.

As we drew closer to the stage, David's eyes and mine locked on to each other.

Oh, my love, I thought.

Tears were streaming down his face. He didn't weep or sob as I entered the sanctuary and approached him; rather, tears fell down his face like a water faucet that couldn't be turned off. He was even smiling as the tears fell.

As my dad and I stood next to the steps leading up to the platform, we shared one of my last hugs with him as a single young woman. My dad hugged David and placed my hand in his. We walked up the steps to find our place on stage. Tears were still flowing down his face. I wiped his tears with my hand.

I scanned the audience and was thrilled to see our senior pastor and friends there and to see my family and David's family sitting in the front row. We knew that those who were unable to attend were watching us through the online live stream.

The associate pastor welcomed everyone to our wedding ceremony and announced that David and I desired to have a time of worship with our guests. Our ceremony began with a time of praising our Savior. We held hands and worshiped the One who is worthy of all our adoration.

Through David's tears and praise, his smile continued shining. I looked around and was happy to see everyone around us worshiping Christ. As the last song concluded, our pastor led us in prayer. I wiped the stream of tears from my soon-to-be husband's face.

In my blissful state, staring into my love's eyes, the associate pastor shared three principles that would help and guide us on our journey of marriage: commitment, the marriage vows, and Jesus Christ. He explained that commitment demands sacrifice and hard work, which would entail putting ourselves aside and caring for the other, until death parts us.

"Why are the marriage vows so important?" He asked rhetorically. "Because this is exactly what Jesus did for us. For better *and* for worse, He is with us. While we're abounding and when we are not, Jesus is with us. Whether we're sick or healthy, Jesus is with us. He loved us and cherished us until His death on the cross. That's why Paul compared marriage with the relationship Jesus has with the church. He values marriage and looks at marriage in the same manner in which Christ came to earth to die for the church."

He continued, "The biblical purpose of marriage is God-centered. Because it's a divine institution, it is always—*always*—centered in Jesus Christ. Your marriage is meant to point to the truth of the crucified and risen Savior, and by the grace of God your marriage is meant to be the most faithful reflection of that relationship you can possibly be.

"The success or failure of your marriage is going to be determined and predicated upon your own personal relationship with God. Keep your relationship with God strong. When your relationship with God is strong, when you're both walking committedly, wholeheartedly, dedicatedly with God, you're going to have a great marriage—not a perfect marriage, but you're going to have a wonderful and good marriage. While commitment and love are the building blocks for your marriage, Jesus is the foundation that brings everything together in harmony in your relationship as husband and wife. If you build your marriage on anything else—money, success, your family, your future—your foundation will have no strength, no permanence, no security, no stability."

His message was resounding powerfully in the background as I gazed into my love's eyes.

Then it was time to say our marriage vows. David said his vows first, then it was my turn. And then came the phrase I longed to hear: "You may now kiss your bride!" We held one another and kissed before God and man as a testimony of our lifelong covenant to one another.

"It is my privilege to present to you Mr. and Mrs. David Akana!" The associate pastor proclaimed. We turned to our guests and let out a shout as our upbeat getaway song resounded through the speakers:

> This is amazing grace, this is unfailing love!
> That you would take my place,
> that you would bear my cross.

> You laid down Your life that I would be set free.
> Oh, Jesus, I sing for all that You've done for me![18]

David high-fived people as we made our way to the sanctuary door, and I lifted my bouquet into the air.

"We're finally married!" David exclaimed as we entered the foyer.

"Yes, finally!" I said. I could hardly believe that the precious gift of marriage was now ours.

We received hugs and congratulations in the foyer. I walked over to the table where we had our nontraditional guest book. It was a flat map of the world with a verse on top: "Go therefore and make disciples of all the nations" (Matthew 28:19). I envisioned the piece of art hanging up in our home.

Then, without any time to spare, our wedding planner ushered us out of the church into the limo that awaited us. David's brother, the best man, treated us with a special ride to the afternoon luncheon.

David and I sat in the very back of the limo. David looked at me with wonder and deep love in his eyes. Our foreheads met together. All the world disappeared around us as we savored those first moments of marriage. We enjoyed the plush cruise to the golf course. I felt like Cinderella with her prince in a modern-day chariot.

We arrived at the luncheon as a light drizzle of rain began falling. David and I took pictures by a fountain at the golf course and then underneath a canopy of trees where David spun and dipped me to capture our first moments as a married couple. We went inside the building, and the emcee began to introduce our wedding party. We enjoyed fellowshipping with our guests and a delicious meal. We thanked everyone for their support.

Then, again without any time to spare, we had to make our way to the exit because we had a flight to catch. I went to a back room and quickly changed out of my wedding dress into a white summer dress.

Leighton and one of our good friends drove us to the airport. Our honeymoon destination was a neighboring island, Kauaʻi. When I was a teenager, I had received a magazine in the mail about Kauaʻi. As I had flipped through the pages of the magazine, the images of the garden island intrigued me. The untouched natural beauty and waterfalls looked like a romantic destination, and the magazine even said it was a popular honeymoon destination.

Little did I know then that my future husband lived on Oʻahu, and that Kauaʻi would be only a short forty-minute plane ride away. David said he was up for an adventure to Kauaʻi. We waved goodbye to the wedding party from our getaway car. We kissed, and I was thrilled that I could finally say, "My beloved is mine and I am his" (Song of Solomon 2:16). We arrived at the airport, said goodbye, and made our way into the terminal.

Walking in the airport felt surreal after having just been married a few hours prior. We went through security and found our gate. Near our gate were a few massage chairs, so David and I planted ourselves in the chairs. Shortly after our massage, the flight crew announced that we would begin boarding. We boarded and took our seats.

I sat next to *my husband.*

On so many plane rides, I had traveled alone. So many times, I had longed for him to be next to me. Now he was no longer an ocean away. On this short plane ride, he was next to me holding my hand. His tears had dried, and now his eyes reflected only sheer excitement.

Shortly after the plane reached optimal altitude, it began descending. After deplaning, we made our way to the airport's rental car area, and a lady at the counter congratulated us on our very recent marriage.

"Wait, you two are *kama'aina*?" She asked us. *Kama'aina* literally translates as "of the land," and it's the term used for Hawaiian residents, a status that qualifies for a discount at many businesses.

"Yes, we are!" David replied.

"If you want to upgrade to a Mustang convertible, it would be fifteen dollars more a day," she said. We looked at each other and quickly agreed. She handed us the keys.

We made our way to the parking lot and found our red Mustang convertible. We jumped in, and while I didn't think David could be more thrilled, he seemed to exhibit even more joy. He looked around the dashboard and felt for the different switches; soon he had a feel for the car. Before I knew it, we were cruising down the one main highway in Kaua'i.

"It's a beast waiting to be unleashed," David remarked. He unleashed it a bit, and we flew for a few moments like a wild stallion down the highway toward our hotel.

While I didn't shed any tears during our ceremony, tears did flow that night. On the night that we became one, I was overwhelmed by God's faithfulness. David thought something was wrong. No, nothing was wrong. In fact, by God's grace, everything was right. It was a promise fulfilled—a promise made to a seventeen-year-old girl. A promise made to every man and woman that while disobedience brings curses, obedience brings blessing. I was overtaken with the reality of the great faithfulness of our God.

Reflection

- Have you ever been overwhelmed by the faithfulness of God? Is there an area in your life that you need to see His faithfulness?

- Write out a prayer thanking Him for His faithfulness, and for the faith to continue trusting Him.

Meditation

Know therefore that the Lord your God is God; he is the faithful God, keeping his covenant of love to a thousand generations of those who love him and keep his commandments (Deuteronomy 7:9).

If you are willing and obedient, you shall eat the good of the land (Isaiah 1:19).

If we are faithless, he remains faithful—for he cannot deny himself (2 Timothy 2:13).

Chapter Fourteen

Agapé Love

I will build my life upon your love;
it is a firm foundation.
(Pat Barrett)

I held on to my husband's hand as we made our way around the island with the Mustang convertible top down. I looked up to the mountains covered in lush green vegetation that cascaded down to deep valleys; it was pristine, untouched beauty. I looked at my new hubby. He continued beaming as he gripped the steering wheel.

"Get ready, wifey," David said. I threw my hands into the air as David tested the car's unruly power. A rush of fresh air surged by as we flew down the narrow highway.

"I want us to be a married couple whose honeymoon never ends," David said, as the car settled into a steady pace.

"Yes!" I exclaimed. "Let's be like that married couple we saw at the restaurant."

Earlier we had seen an older couple sitting next to each other, and as she sat next to him, she rested her head on his shoulder. After all the many years they had together, it appeared that she still wanted to be as close as possible to her man. While we could sense their unity, it was impossible to grasp their trials, joys, valleys, and mountaintops that had forged their marriage and tested their vows.

We turned off the highway down a gravel road, and after a few miles arrived at a densely forested area and looked up at a sign: *Outfitters Kauai.*

"We've arrived!" I exclaimed. David smiled and put the car in park. We walked over to the check-in table and received instructions with a small group. After securing our helmets, the instructor brought over a gorgeous bay gelding. Strength and beauty permeated my sturdy horse. I reached out to stroke his forehead.

David was given Cash, an easygoing chestnut quarter horse. We mounted our horses and strategically stayed behind the group. When our instructor wasn't looking, we squeezed our horses' sides to catch up. I gripped the reins as my body jolted rhythmically with the creature's massive strides.

Finally, we arrived at the ziplining station. Butterflies welled in my stomach as I gazed at our launch pad. The crew secured our horses to a halter hitch, then we climbed three flights of stairs. We arrived at the apex and hopped into a harness. After checking the cables and steel hooks, they swung us horizontal to the ground and thrusted us forward. We soared high above a valley—superman style, side by side. A rush of adrenaline surged through my veins as we temporarily possessed the superhuman power to fly.

After our adventure, we drove to Kaua'i Coffee Plantation, the largest coffee farm in the United States. We went into the quaint coffee shop and ordered fresh blended iced coffee. We grabbed our drinks and followed signs to the coffee maze behind the store.

A narrow path weaved through acreage covered in coffee trees. Along the path, signs were posted with jokes and with information about coffee. One sign read: *What did the depressed coffee say? Pour me, pour me.* We laughed and read another sign: *Coffee grounds are not supposed to be refrigerated.*

We stood on the side of the path and turned toward one another. "Then why do so many people refrigerate their coffee grounds?" I asked. At the same moment—and in the exact same tone—we both said, "They just don't know." We gasped in unison. We continued looking at each other, surprised. Our first week of marriage unveiled an entirely new depth of unity.

When we got back to O'ahu, we went to a bank and merged our finances into one account. Our paychecks would be deposited in this account, and we understood that all financial purchases would now be in consideration of the other spouse. Moreover, every trial and every joy would be together. We became Team Akana.

I had created a vision for this team as a wide-eyed teenage girl when I had signed a commitment to wait for my future husband. In essence, I believed that we would get married and then jump into the happily-ever-after scene that was portrayed at the end of every fairy tale. This vision failed to consider the reality that my spouse and I are both sinners—saved by grace, but still two imperfect individuals. I had never considered that our life of soaring above mountains might also include trudging through deep valleys.

Displaying God's love and grace sounded easy and doable, especially on the day we looked deep into each other's eyes and said, "For better *and* for worse." Standing on the summit of our wedding day, I had no idea of the vast amount of grace needed by sinners (including myself)—until I became one flesh with one man and lived under one roof with him. As Elisabeth Elliot said, "You know that all have sinned and fallen short of the glory of God, and this includes your husband who comes short, also, of some of the glories you expected to find in him."[19]

One Saturday evening at One Love, the pastor taught through Acts 27. Paul was in chains for preaching the gospel and was being brought to Rome to be tried by King Herod Agrippa. The ship was harbored at Fair Havens on the island of Crete, but when "a south wind blew softly," the crew decided to sail against Paul's instructions (27:13). Soon, storm clouds and a tempestuous wind surged in and began to toss the ship around the Mediterranean Sea. After fourteen days and nights, no one had eaten, and the crew feared that their lives would be taken. Paul then reassured the crew that they would all survive because an angel of God had appeared to him with that message (27:24). Then, on the fifteenth day, they ran the ship aground. They jumped off, swam toward land, and arrived safely on shore (28:1). The wind and waves ceased, and the sun eventually broke through the dark clouds.

"Every person here is either in a storm, about to go in one, or on the other side of one," the pastor said to the congregation. *Yikes!* I thought. *Are storms that prevalent?* I would soon find out that they are.

Four weeks into our marriage, I experienced something that seemed more like a hurricane. After work one day, I grabbed David's phone to see if his mom had gotten back to him about plans for the weekend. A text message notification had lit up his phone's screen. I read it, but it didn't make sense; it looked like street slang. I googled the phrase, and my heart nearly stopped. *No, my husband doesn't do drugs or sell them. I didn't marry a druggie; I married a man of God, and He lives by what he teaches.* Shards of confusion launched into my heart, and I feared future treachery.

A few weeks later, I learned that my husband had two bachelor parties, one with Christian friends and one with co-workers at a strip club. Betrayal cut the deep corners of my heart. I confronted David with tears and confusion. Later, I laid on our bed and journaled:

> Lord, forgive me for being unloving toward David. Reassure him that he will rise. Take away lustful desires and pride. You have given us the name Warriors—so now give us the shield of faith, the breastplate of righteousness, the helmet of salvation, and shod our feet with the Gospel of peace. In Jesus' name.

We stepped down from ministry and began to focus our energies on building the foundation of our marriage. I figured that as long as we remained faithful to one another, we could work through everything and have our happily-ever-after marriage. Paul wrote the following in 2 Corinthians 11:2-3,

> For I feel a divine jealousy for you, since I betrothed you to one husband, to present you as a pure virgin to Christ. But I am afraid that as the serpent deceived Eve by his cunning, your thoughts will be led astray from a sincere and pure devotion to Christ.

Paul desired to find simplicity and purity in the congregation, and I desired to find this in my marriage.

David began working long hours at work. And in the coming months, I spent many evenings on our couch or in our bed waiting for him. I texted and called my husband at 8:00 p.m., 9:00 p.m., 10:00 p.m., asking when he would be home. I learned that many "late nights at work" were actually evenings of drinking with co-workers and hanging out with an old high school friend.

One night my husband didn't come home and I found his car in a sketchy neighborhood in Nu'uanu. I waited for him and found God's strength in remembering the times He had come through for me before. Nefarious activity flooded the area, but I had this overwhelming sense that God was over it all. Later I read in Proverbs, "The eyes of the LORD are in every place, keeping watch on the evil and the good" (Proverbs 15:3). When my husband appeared from around the corner, I sensed His Spirit urging me to pour out grace as Jesus did to the woman caught in sin (John 8). Instead, I reacted out of my pain and so we sat in the parking lot as two broken individuals. I didn't understand how it was possible to proclaim Christ and then live opposite of everything He lived and died for. Jesus warns of this double standard:

> Beware of false prophets who come to you in sheep's clothing, but inwardly are ravenous wolves. You will recognize them by their fruits. Are grapes gathered from thornbushes, or figs from thistles? So, every healthy tree bears good fruit, but the diseased tree bears bad fruit (Matthew 7:15-17 NKJV).

Scripture also says that a friend of the world is an enemy of

God, that a double-minded man is unstable in all of his ways, and that freshwater and saltwater cannot come from the same vessel (James 4:4; 1:8; 3:11-12). I felt like I was on a boat tossed around on an unpredictable ocean. *Aren't we supposed to battle darkness outside the home, not within the sanctuary of home?* My heart felt tattered and broken. *Isn't my husband supposed to love me and come home to me? Why does he lie and deceive me?* Soon we would find that living for Jesus *and* living in darkness is, in fact, impossible.

In the middle of storms, I tended to react out of my pain—not out of the peace that God gives. Jesus was the ultimate example when He held His peace and trusted God in the face of tremendous opposition (Matthew 26:63). Later I came to realize that when Christ says to take on His mindset, this should apply even in the midst of betrayal and hardships (1 Corinthians 2:16). As Peter said:

> But when you do good and suffer, if you take it patiently, this is commendable before God. For to this you were called, because Christ suffered for us, leaving us an example, that we should follow in His steps (1 Peter 2:20b-21 NKJV).

I desperately needed stability in my marriage, and although at times, I failed to respond with the wisdom and grace my husband needed, the Lord was my rock who kept me from being swallowed up. As the Psalmist declared, "If it had not been the LORD who was on our side when people rose up against us, they would have swallowed us up alive" (Psalm 124:2-3).

Just as Elisabeth Elliot said that there's an enemy of our souls who hates purity, we know that this same adversary despises marriage. One night I had a dream about my husband. In my dream,

David and I were in the midst of a huge crowd of people, and we were all running for our lives. Suddenly a massive lion came into view, and it pounced on David. I stopped running, and a verse flashed into my mind: "Be sober, be vigilant; because your adversary the devil walks about like a roaring lion, seeking whom he may devour" (1 Peter 5:8 NKJV). I woke up from my dream and felt an urgency to pray for my husband. I came to realize that sin from David's past had never been put to death; rather, it had been hidden. And while God in His mercy was bringing it to light to be cleansed, Satan was also at work to destroy David, our ministry, and our marriage. Ephesians 6 gives clear instructions on how to engage in spiritual warfare and to win. And in verse 18, we're told to pray at all times.

At my wedding shower, I had received a book titled *The Power of a Praying Wife*. Each chapter is named after a specific subject that the wife would pray for regarding her husband. I spent mornings on our bed praying for my husband's work, finances, attitude, priorities, mind, and faith. Sometimes when I opened the book, the topic seemed to be exactly what David needed prayer for. This book provided a practical way to lift up the one I love most to the throne of God. And when I finished the book, I realized I had essentially prayed for my man from his head to his toes.

Despite our challenges, David and I had many beautiful times together. I loved running into his warm embrace after work and "let him kiss me with the kisses of his mouth" (Song of Solomon 1:2). We went skydiving together, swam with sharks, and ventured to Japan and Disneyland. We shared lots of laughter and adventures together. I knew that he loved me, and I loved him; however, God needed to cultivate a *deeper* love in our hearts—an *agapé love*. *Agapé* is a Greek word that describes the highest form of love that's willing to lay down one's life for the welfare of another. This love "does not seek its own, is not provoked, thinks no evil; does not rejoice in iniquity, but rejoices in the truth; bears all things, believes all things, hopes all things, endures all things" (1 Corinthians 13:5-6 NKJV).

One Sunday evening we ventured to the west side of the island. It was a special weekend for us because it was the final weekend before entering into our second year of marriage together. As the earth silently and faithfully spun on its axis in space, the sun vibrantly kissed our atmosphere and set the sea on fire. David and I battled three-foot waves that perpetually rolled in. Suddenly, the peak of the waves became translucent and burned with the sun's rays before breaking and crashing into the shore. We ducked under the sunlit waves and marveled at God's glory. These beautiful moments reminded me of Psalm 84:11: "For the LORD God is a sun and shield; the LORD bestows favor and honor. No good thing does he withhold from those who walk uprightly."

However, Scripture also warns about a divided house. As Jesus says in Mark 3:25, "And if a house is divided against itself, that house will not be able to stand." Even though we had beautiful times together, I spent countless evenings and nights wondering where my husband was and what He was doing.

My brother Justin told me one day, "That would be strange to not know where your spouse is."

"I hear what you're saying, but that sounds so foreign to me," I replied. "This is all I've known."

I prayed desperately for David and for our marriage during these challenging times. We met with the associate pastor a couple of times for counsel. I met weekly with my best friend and matron of honor, Arianna, to pray together. At times it felt like I was barely hanging on, but I held on to hope that this was just a season and that things would get better. As Christian said as he climbed the Hill of Difficulty in *The Pilgrim's Progress*:

> This hill, though high, I covet to ascend; the difficulty will not me offend, for I perceive the way to life lies here. Come, pluck up, heart, let's neither faint nor fear. Better, though difficult, the right way to go, than wrong, though easy, where the end is woe.[20]

Reflection

- In what ways are you building your life on Jesus? Is there anything that is hindering you from building your life on Christ?

- Write out a prayer asking God to help you build your life on the rock of His Word and His ways and to remove anything that may be getting in the way.

Meditation

You shall love the LORD your God with all your heart and with all your soul and with all your might (Deuteronomy 6:5).

See, I am setting before you today a blessing and a curse: the blessing, if you obey the commandments of the LORD your God, which I command you today, and the curse, if you do not obey the commandments of the LORD your God, but turn aside from the way that I am commanding you today, to go after other gods that you have not known (Deuteronomy 11:26-28).

Thus says the LORD: "Cursed is the man who trusts in man and makes flesh his strength, whose heart turns away from the LORD. He is like a shrub in the desert, and shall not see any good come. He shall dwell in the parched places of the wilderness, in an uninhabited salt land. "Blessed is the man who trusts in the LORD, whose trust is the LORD. He is like a tree planted by water, that sends out its roots by the stream, and does not fear when heat comes, for its leaves remain green, and is not anxious in the year of drought, for it does not cease to bear fruit" (Jeremiah 17:5-8).

Chapter Fifteen

Faithful, You Are

Who is this king of glory? The LORD, *strong and mighty, the* LORD *mighty in battle.*
(PSALM 24:8)

"Hi, hubby!" I answered my phone. "Are you done with work?" It was 2:50 p.m., ten minutes before David's scheduled shift was over.

"Hi, wifey! No, I'll actually be working late today. I should be done at 6:00 p.m.," he said.

"Okay," I replied. "Dinner will be ready at 6:30 p.m. I'll be making steak for us!"

"Awesome! Well, I better get back to work," he said.

"See you later. I love you!" I exclaimed.

"Love you too! Bye." We hung up.

I went home and made dinner. I set the asparagus and steak on the stovetop and went to our living room to watch some YouTube videos. Six o'clock turned into 7:00 p.m. Our meal became cold as it sat on the stovetop. *Another late evening.* I sent a text. And later, I called him.

No answer. However, at 8:50 p.m., the spiritual realm met the physical. I received a phone call from David. Light collided with darkness in the same powerful way that warm air collides with cold air to create a storm.

"Hi, David!"

I could hear loud singing and music in the background.

"David?" It appeared that he had pocket-dialed me.

My heart sank. *He's with his co-workers again.* It sounded like my husband, but a different version of him. Cuss words and blasphemy flowed freely from his mouth. It was as if God came down from the storm clouds as a mighty warrior to expose the unfruitful works of darkness that are done in secret (Ephesians 5:11-12).

I knelt down on our bedroom floor. *Lord, make me invisible. If there's anything else that needs to be revealed, You reveal it.* I clasped on to my phone and waited. *After he's done carousing with his co-workers, he will come home to me,* I reasoned.

An hour passed by. One co-worker said that he heard from "the boss," so he needed to leave. It appeared that others were leaving as well.

Then sexual perversity tainted my husband's language, and a destructive plan was devised. *No, Lord, no! Protect my marriage!*

"David! David!" I yelled into my phone. Suddenly we were disconnected. Daggers sliced my soul at a depth I didn't know was possible. I dropped my phone and ran into the kitchen. My mind felt like it might snap, and I couldn't catch my breath. A sacred covenant meant to exemplify God's love and goodness was about to be defiled, as if its worth was less than the mire in a pig's pen (2 Peter 2:22).

What am I supposed to do? I didn't know where he was. The enemy came in like a flood: *Your life is over, just kill yourself.*

No, no, no! The Spirit of the Lord pierced through the darkness: *Call Wendy.*

I ran back into our bedroom and grabbed my phone from the floor. I called the woman who had planned our wedding and who had also been mentoring me the past few weeks.

"Wendy!" I shouted through my panic. "It's David! He pocket-dialed me! He's about to defile our marriage! I don't know what to do!"

"We need to pray!" she said. "Kristine, you pray first!"

"Lord, please forgive me for my lack of trust. Lord, protect our marriage bed! Rise up and defend my marriage!" Suddenly floodgates opened, and I began to sob. Without hesitation, Wendy took over. She prayed like I had never been prayed over before. And as she prayed, peace seemed to infuse my soul. My breathing slowed, and the tears stopped.

"Amen!" she said.

"Amen," I said.

"Are you okay now?" she asked.

"Yes," I replied. We hung up. I hopped into my car, determined to find my husband. I searched bars, karaoke joints, and strip clubs. I felt like I needed to call someone to help me, but I knew that there was no police or assistance for this kind of situation. I needed help from the greatest warrior. As Psalm 121:2 declares, "My help comes from the Lord, who made heaven and earth".

I went home and pored over Scripture all night. His Word was like soothing oil on my soul:

> "For this reason God gave them up to vile passions. For even their women exchanged the natural use for what is against nature... But we have the mind of Christ... Watch, stand fast in the faith, be brave, be strong. Let all that you do be done with love... And He said to me, my grace is sufficient for you, for my strength is made perfect in weakness" (Romans 1:26; 1 Corinthians 2:16 and 16:13; 2 Corinthians 12:9 NKJV).

His love and comfort sustained me through the night (Psalm 86:13). The darkness gave way to dawn, and as I searched for answers, I deeply wept over what could have been and how this was never supposed to happen. I grieved the loss of my husband—the man my soul loved. I called him again and again and again. I sent him texts and emails, to no avail.

I put my phone aside and flipped through my Bible and read about the time leading up to Jesus' death and resurrection. He told His disciples that He would die, but that after three days He would come back to life (Matthew 20:17-19). I felt that three days after the betrayal, something significant would happen. *He will return my calls,* I reasoned.

He didn't call; instead, three days later, as I drove from my place to the cellular store, I sensed a supernatural healing in my soul. The pain—deep, aching pain—had lifted. I knew that Jesus carried my sorrows and infirmities so I wouldn't have to carry them (Isaiah 53:4).

As I continued driving, I heard a still, small voice: *Do you think this is too hard for Me to forgive?* Suddenly I knew that this sin, like every sin, could also be washed away. Furthermore, I was given the miraculous ability to forgive David, and I knew it was because my

Savior had forgiven me. As a great hymn says: "Jesus paid it all, all to Him I owe; sin had left a crimson stain; He washed it white as snow." All these things happened in a matter of moments.

The next day I went to church and met with the senior pastor afterward. Pastor Derald sat across a table from me. It was two years and three months after our marriage ceremony in the same church. My eyes were glazed over with tears after I shared about what had happened a few days prior. He said, "If you turn to James 3, I think that will shed some light on your situation." He began to read:

> "But if you have bitter envy and self-seeking in your hearts, do not boast and lie against the truth. This wisdom does not descend from above, but is earthly, sensual, demonic. For where envy and self-seeking exist, confusion and every evil thing are there." (vv.14-16 NKJV)

He continued: "I bet you were confused a lot these past two years."

"Yes, I was," I replied. I stared at the Scripture in front of me and thought about the instability that marked our marriage.

"This is not your fault," he said. "To be envious of evil men's ways, to be bitter toward you, and to seek one's own way led to a downward progression of earthly, sensual, and demonic ways," he explained.

As if a spotlight beamed down from heaven, truth came and lit up my confusion. I didn't understand how he could do this to me, how this could happen to our marriage, and how this could happen in the church—until now. We had vowed to forsake all others and be committed to one another until death. However, this downward progression ultimately led to a violation of our marriage bed. Proverbs 6 and 7 warn spouses against this destructive path: "Do not let your heart turn aside to her ways, do not stray into her paths; her house is the way to hell descending to the chambers of death" (7:25, 27 NKJV).

"What are you going to do?" Pastor Derald asked me.

"I'm going to leave," I responded.

"And you have every right to leave. There are reasons God permits divorce under these circumstances. And one of them is to protect the spouse from deadly diseases," he said. Pastor Derald encouraged me to press into God. "Psalms is very comforting," he told me.

I pressed into His Word and searched for more answers. I meditated on 2 Corinthians 4:17: "For this light momentary affliction is preparing for us an eternal weight of glory beyond all comparison." I knew that Paul's life was filled with shipwrecks, imprisonments, and beatings; he was even left for dead. Despite these great challenges, Paul considered them "light and momentary," and I desired to take on the same mindset. Isaiah says in 43:8 that when we pass through waters, God will be with us. He is a loving father who will never leave us, even as the waters surge. And we are to set our minds on things that are above, not on things that are on earth (Galatians 3:2). These verses were spiritual life rafts for me. Any time I felt like I was sinking, God would lift me up.

Later that week, my five-year-old nephew caught wind of what had happened to us and pulled me aside at Jamba Juice, our favorite smoothie shop in Hawai'i.

"Does David still love you?" he asked me. His eyes were wide and filled with innocence.

"Yes, he does," I replied. "And I love him too. Do you know why I love him? It's because someone else loves him. Who else loves him?" I looked at my seven-year-old niece.

She took a moment, and then shouted, "Jesus!"

"That's right! Jesus loves him. And we don't need to talk about what happened. We just need to pray for him."

I gathered my niece and nephew on the sidewalk outside Jamba Juice, and we prayed for David. I knew that we were able to love because Jesus first loved us (1 John 4:11).

I had mourned the loss of my husband and our marriage; now what brings me to tears is God's great love. He rose up as a mighty warrior and defended me that night by holding my heart (Exodus 14:14). Without His love, my afflictions would overwhelm me, I would be alone going through the waters, and I would have nothing to lift my gaze to. Moreover, I would be lost forever. Instead, I am eternally loved and forgiven. As another great hymn says: "The love of God is greater far than tongue or pen can ever tell. It goes beyond the highest star and reaches to the lowest hell."

A few days later, on my last day in Hawai'i, I went to my favorite beach and jumped into the ocean, letting wave after wave wash over me. I swam to the peak of a wave and let its power propel me closer to shore. I began to tread water as I gazed at the infinite ocean, drawing in its depths. I realized what had happened wasn't part of God's perfect design, but I could trust the One whose grace and faithfulness is greater and deeper than the wondrous depths of the ocean He had lovingly created. "And now Lord, what do I wait for? My hope is in You" Psalm 39:7.

I wonder sometimes if David knows how much He is loved. Before the foundations of the earth, He was called for a purpose.

Friendship with the world is enmity with God, but there is great hope in true repentance. As Proverbs 28:13 says, "Whoever conceals his transgressions will not prosper, but he who confesses and forsakes them will obtain mercy." Does He know that God came to crush his enemy who is working hard to destroy him—and that He came to undo the power of sin in his life? Jesus' blood was spilt so he could be forgiven and live *abundantly* here on earth and *eternally* with Him in heaven.

So many people need this message, and it is up to us to tell them. As we follow Christ, He graciously chooses to make His appeal through these jars of clay. As Paul said:

> We have this treasure in earthen vessels, so that the surpassing greatness of the power will be of God and not from ourselves... Now then, we are ambassadors for Christ, as though God were pleading through us: we implore you on Christ's behalf, be reconciled to God (2 Corinthians 4:7; 2 Corinthians 5:20 NKJV).

God is our salvation, and *missions* is our calling. Let's go for God and love one another. "For with the LORD there is mercy, and with Him is abundant redemption" (Psalm 130:7 NKJV).

Reflection

- How have you seen God's love in your life? If you could sum up your life mission in one sentence, what would it be?

- Write out a prayer asking God to guide you and for Him to receive all the glory in your life.

Meditation

Now to him who is able to do far more abundantly than all that we ask or think, according to the power at work within us, to him be glory in the church and in Christ Jesus throughout all generations, forever and ever. Amen (Ephesians 3:20-21).

Therefore, preparing your minds for action, and being sober-minded, set your hope fully on the grace that will be brought to you at the revelation of Jesus Christ (1 Peter 1:13).

And we know that for those who love God all things work together for good, for those who are called according to his purpose (Romans 8:28).

Afterword

It is God's will that every man comes to salvation and that no one should perish (2 Peter 3:9). But God will never overstep the free will of man—for love without the freedom or right to respond is no love at all.

Christ proves His love for us in that while we were yet sinners, Christ died for us (Romans 5:8). While we were rebelling against God, He sent His Son to die a horrific death to pay the ransom for our eternal souls (Isaiah 53). Who can fathom this great love? If we turn from our sin and surrender to Him, He promises us eternal life (John 3:17). If we continue in our rebellion, pride, and immorality, He will allow us to walk that dreadful path, and we will certainly reap what we sow—and there are eternal ramifications (1 Corinthians 6:9).

It's tragic that thousands of people every day slip into a dark and hopeless eternity, forever separated from their loving Creator and Savior (Matthew 25:30). It's tragic when our human will encounters the face of God, turns from Him, chooses sin, and allows the enemy to ravage our life (Hebrews 6:4-6; 2 Peter 2:20-22). As C. S. Lewis said:

> It would seem that our Lord finds our desires not too strong, but too weak. We are half-hearted creatures, fooling about with drink and sex and ambition when infinite joy is offered us, like an ignorant child who wants to go on making mud pies in a slum because he cannot imagine what is meant by the offer of a holiday at the sea. We are far too easily pleased.[21]

Will you turn from your sin and surrender to His great love?

If you have surrendered to Christ, then I encourage you to read your Bible diligently and to pray and fast regularly (Hebrews 4:12; Matthew 6:16). These are spiritual disciplines that will strengthen your walk with Christ. Also, it is vital to be part of a church that stands on the Word of God (Hebrews 10:25). Pray for a godly friend, and seek out a godly mentor who will sharpen you, pray with you, and encourage you to go hard after Christ (Proverbs 27:17). I encourage you to look up John MacArthur, John Piper, DLM Christian Lifestyle, and Torch of Christ Ministries on YouTube.

Arianna wrote a poem about how to respond when people mistreat us:

Kind, sweet, and big-hearted.
To the narcissist I was a big target.
Pain and regret because of my naïve ways.
Never realizing those who wounded me didn't even get fazed.
The coldness is unbelievable, it left me amazed.

I pray for my enemies:
Father, correct and help them turn from their error and ways.
Give them mercy, new hearts, and new names.
Forgive, heal, and move forward. All of my burdens to put on your shoulders.
I hear your tender Holy Spirit say:
Keep being kind, sweet, and big-hearted. Look to Christ and see the new chapter He started.
Now You're teaching me to be bold and assertive.
Wisdom in me You have molded.
I can see your story in my life being unfolded.
Thank you Father for your love that is much greater than all of my wounds.
I can see your hand in my life continue to move.
So I ask you Lord, fill my heart with your love, there's plenty of room.
I trust that there is nothing You can't do.
So I ask you Jesus, may all bitterness and unforgiveness in my soul forever be removed.
Once again I can hear your tender Holy Spirit say:
Don't stop being kind, sweet, and big-hearted.
Fear not, your walk with Jesus will forever be guarded.
Year after year, trial after trial, I see You transforming me, even when I'm broken and saddened.
Lord, I trust your beautiful promise that You'll finish what You started.
And by your grace, I will continue to be kind, sweet, and big-hearted.[22]

I would love to hear from you! You can write me on the following page, or email me: missionarynurse89@gmail.com.

Kristine Akana
28910 600th ave.
Warroad, MN. 56763

Notes

Chapter 3: Sex, Purity, and Relationships

1. "The Rise in Divorce and Cohabitation: Is There a Link?" US National Library of Medicine National Institutes of Health, June 5, 2017, https://www.ncbi.nlm.nih.gov/pmc/articles/PMC5518209/.
2. Pam Stenzel and Crystal Kirgiss, *Sex Has a Price Tag* (Grand Rapids: Zondervan, 2015).
3. Stenzel and Kirgiss, *Sex Has a Price Tag*, 7.
4. Stenzel and Kirgiss, *Sex Has a Price Tag*, 10.
5. Karen Rogstad, *ABC of Sexually Transmitted Infections*, 6th edition (West Sussex UK: Blackwell Publishing Ltd., 2011), 1.
6. "Counterintuitive Trends in the Link Between Premarital Sex and Marital Stability," Institute for Family Studies, June 6, 2016, https://ifstudies.org/blog/counterintuitive-trends-in-the-link-between-premarital-sex-and-marital-stability.
7. Steve Rudd, "Ancient Jewish Three-Stage Wedding Customs," http://www.bible.ca/marriage/ancient-jewish-three-stage-weddings-and-marriage-customs-ceremony-in-the-bible.htm.

Chapter 7: Throwing Rocks

8. Ana Gonzalez, "Slave Revolt: The Creation of Haiti," https://www.stmuhistorymedia.org/slave-revolt-the-creation-of-haiti/.

Chapter 8: Difficult Surrender

9. Copyright © 2003 Sony/ATV Music Publishing LLC and Driver's Ed Music All Rights Administered by Sony/ATV Music Publishing LLC, 424 Church Street, Suite 1200, Nashville, TN 37219 International Copyright Secured All Rights Reserved. Reprinted by Permission of Hal Leonard LLC.

Chapter 10: An Unexpected Meeting

10. Samuel Kamakau, *Ruling Chiefs of Hawaii.* (Honolulu, Kamehameha School Press, 1961), 92-104.
11. Peter Pirie, "The Consequences of Cook's Hawaiian Contacts on the Local Population," https://core.ac.uk/download/pdf/5103891.pdf.
12. Chris Cook, "Henry Opukaha'ia of Hawaii," http://across.co.nz/HO208.html.
13. Kamakau, *Ruling Chiefs of Hawaii*, 222.
14. John Kalei Laimana JR., "The Phenomenal Rise to Literacy in Hawai'i Hawaiian Society in the Early Nineteenth Century," https://scholarspace.manoa.hawaii.edu/bitstream/10125/101531/1/Laimana_John_r.pdf.

Chapter 11: This Man

15. Elisabeth Elliot, *Passion and Purity* (Grand Rapids: Fleming H. Revell, 2002), 73.
16. Elliot, *Passion and Purity*, 29.

Chapter 13: A Sacred Covenant

17. Copyright © 2014 Thankyou Music (PRS) (adm. worldwide at CapitolCMGPublishing.com excluding Europe which is adm. by Integrity Music, part of the David C. Cook family. Songs@integritymusic.com) All rights reserved. Used by permission.
18. Copyright © 2013 Essential Music Publishing LLC, a Unit of Sony Music Entertainment (adm. at EssentialMusicPublishing.com). All rights reserved. Used by permission.

Chapter 14: Agapé Love

19. Elisabeth Elliot, *Let Me Be a Woman* (Carol Stream: Tyndale House Publishers, 1976), 72.
20. John Bunyan, *The Pilgrim's Progress* (Grand Rapids: Zondervan Publishing House, 1678), 55.

Afterword

21. C. S. Lewis, *The Weight of Glory* (New York: Macmillan Publishing Company, 1939), 26.
22. Arianna Vargas, "Forgive, Heal, and Move Forward (Don't Stop Being Kind, Sweet, and Big-Hearted", PoetryPoem, 2020, https://poetrypoem.com/cgi-bin/index.pl?poemnumber=1308794&sitename=poet202057&poemoffset=0&displaypoem=t&item=poetry

Order Information

To order additional copies of this book, please visit
www.redemption-press.com.
Also available on Amazon.com and BarnesandNoble.com
or by calling toll-free 1-844-2REDEEM.

CPSIA information can be obtained
at www.ICGtesting.com
Printed in the USA
LVHW081203130221
679242LV00016B/635

9 781646 451739